Presented To
Cedar Mill Community Library

Purchased with a grant
from a 2009 family foundation

Fangs KING COBRAS

The Biggest Venomous Snakes of All!

by Nancy White

Consultant: Raoul Bain, Biodiversity Specialist, Herpetology
Center for Biodiversity and Conservation
American Museum of Natural History
New York, New York

BEARPORT
PUBLISHING

New York, New York

Credits

Cover and Title Page, © Michael D. Kern; TOC, © Martin Harvey/Digital Vision/Getty Images; 4L, © JH Pete Carmichael/Riser/Getty Images; 4R, © David M. Dennis / Animals Animals/Earth Scenes; 5, © Photocyclops.com/SuperStock; 7, © Peter B. Kaplan/Photo Researchers, Inc.; 8, © Sharad Bhandhari/Indiapicture/Alamy; 9, © Snowleopard1/Shutterstock; 10L, © Zoltan Tackas; 10R, © Photocyclops.com/SuperStock; 11, © Omar Ariff/iStockphoto; 12, © Lynn M. Stone/Nature Picture Library; 13, © Mattias Klum/National Geographic/Getty Images; 14, © Belinda Wright/DRK Photo; 15, © Mattias Klum/National Geographic/Getty Images; 16, © C. Huetter/ArcoImages/Peter Arnold Inc.; 17, © David Liebman; 18, Courtesy of Gladys Porter Zoo; 19, Courtesy of Gladys Porter Zoo; 20, Courtesy of Gladys Porter Zoo; 21, © Graham Gary/Newspix/News Ltd/3rd Party Managed Reproduction & Supply Rights; 22, © Mattias Klum/National Geographic Images; 23A, © JH Pete Carmichael/Riser/Getty Images; 23B, © idiz/Shutterstock; 23C, © Snowleopard1/Shutterstock; 23D, © Omar Ariff/iStockphoto; 23E, © Graham Gary/Newspix/News Ltd/3rd Party Managed Reproduction & Supply Rights; 23F, © Photocyclops.com/SuperStock; 23G, © Snowleopard1/Shutterstock; 23H, © Maria Dryfhout/Shutterstock; 24, © Omar Ariff/iStockphoto.

Publisher: Kenn Goin
Senior Editor: Lisa Wiseman
Creative Director: Spencer Brinker
Photo Researcher: Lindsay Blatt
Cover Design: Dawn Beard Creative

Library of Congress Cataloging-in-Publication Data

White, Nancy, 1942–
    King cobras : the biggest venomous snakes of all! / by Nancy White.
        p. cm. — (Fangs)
    Includes bibliographical references and index.
    ISBN-13: 978-1-59716-767-3 (library binding)
    ISBN-10: 1-59716-767-3 (library binding)
    1. King cobra—Juvenile literature. I. Title.
    QL666.O64W45 2009
    597.96'42—c22
                            2008031174

For more information, write to Bearport Publishing Company, Inc., 101 Fifth Avenue, Suite 6R, New York, New York 10003. Printed in the United States of America.

10 9 8 7 6 5 4 3 2 1

Contents

Meet the King

A huge, hungry snake slithers across the dark forest floor. It hasn't eaten in a month, and it's ready for a meal. The deadly hunter lifts its head and silently flicks its forked tongue. Suddenly, it spots what it's looking for—another snake. The killer raises its body up high, ready to **strike**. Its victim better watch out. This is no ordinary snake—it's a king cobra!

The king cobra is the world's largest **venomous** snake. Its bite has enough venom to kill 30 people. Luckily, these creatures hardly ever bite humans. They use their venom mainly when hunting. Their favorite **prey** are snakes, such as pythons, rat snakes, and even other cobras.

◀ Green tree python

Rat snake ▶

King cobra

King cobras are longer than most cars. They can grow to be 18 feet (5.5 m) long and weigh more than 40 pounds (18 kg).

Sneaky Snakes

King cobras are good hunters because they can easily sneak up on other animals. These fierce killers live mostly in tropical **rain forests**. Since their body colors blend in with the forest floor, they can often sneak up on their prey without being seen.

When a king cobra is ready to attack, it does something to make itself look very scary. The snake uses special muscles to spread out the loose neck skin behind its head. This "hood" makes the king cobra's head look even bigger than it really is.

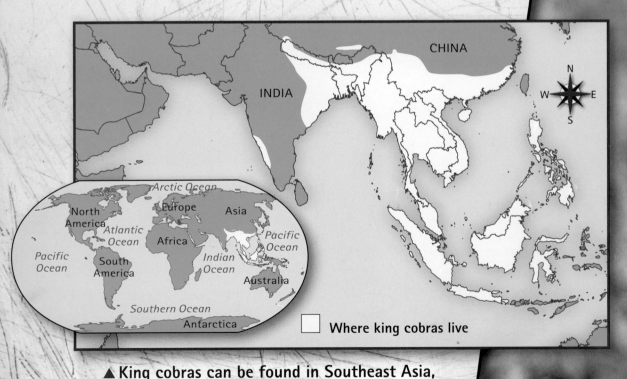

▲ King cobras can be found in Southeast Asia, including northern India and southern China.

Snakes don't have ears on the outside of their heads. However, the bones in their jaws can feel the slight shaking of the ground caused by an animal or person moving nearby.

9

Deadly Poison

While a king cobra uses its senses to hunt, it uses its **fangs** to kill. The fangs are attached to the snake's upper jaw. They are about half an inch (1 cm) long. Like a doctor's needle, they are hollow and sharp. They can easily pierce a victim's skin.

What makes the fangs deadly is the venom that pumps through them. The poison is made in two **sacs,** one on each side of the snake's head. The sacs are connected to the fangs by tubes. The deadly venom shoots out of the sacs, through the tubes, and into the fangs.

Black mamba ▶

▲ Coral snake

With one bite, a king cobra pumps about one teaspoon (5 ml) of venom into its victim. That's more poison than any other venomous snake is able to inject. However, the king cobra's venom is not the strongest. Mambas and coral snakes, for example, make deadlier poison.

The King Strikes

Once a king cobra is ready to bite its victim, it **coils** the lower part of its body. It then raises its upper body high off the ground—up to six feet (1.8 m)! Spreading its hood, the giant hunter opens its mouth wide, flicks its tongue, and strikes! As the fangs sink into the victim, the deadly venom is injected.

If the prey tries to escape, the cobra slithers after it and bites again. The venom causes sharp pain. It makes the victim's muscles and lungs stop working so the animal can't move or breathe.

▲ A king cobra getting ready to attack

A king cobra swims in a stream.

King cobras have many ways to chase their prey. These expert hunters can slither along the ground, swim across rivers, or climb trees to catch a meal.

A Meal for a King

The king cobra doesn't wait for its prey to die before eating it. While the victim is still alive, the snake grabs the animal's head with its teeth and swallows it whole. The prey may not die until it's inside the snake's stomach.

It can take one hour for a king cobra to swallow a large victim. Digesting the whole animal, including its skin and bones, can take a week. The snake may not need to eat again for a month.

▲ A king cobra eating a rat snake

Snakes have teeth, but they can't chew. Instead, the king cobra uses its teeth to grab its victim. Then the snake's jaws move from side to side, pushing the animal down its throat.

Self-Defense

A king cobra won't usually attack unless it's hungry. However, it will defend itself if it's being attacked. First, it tries to frighten the enemy away. The snake raises its head and spreads its hood. It opens its mouth and growls like a dog.

If the enemy isn't scared away, then the snake strikes out with its head. It doesn't always bite. If it does, it may not use venom. It can take about 10 to 15 days to make the poison, so often the snake saves it for killing prey.

A mongoose

Most animals are afraid to attack an adult king cobra. A little animal called the mongoose, however, is one of the snake's few enemies. The mongoose is so quick that it can jump out of the way when a cobra strikes.

A king cobra in a
defense position

The Queen's Nest

In the spring, the female king cobra makes a nest for her eggs. She uses her body to pile up dead leaves and twigs. She lays 20 to 50 eggs on the pile and covers them with more leaves and twigs. Then she coils herself up on top.

Sometimes animals try to eat the king cobra's eggs. The female scares them away by rising up, spreading her hood, and growling. She sits on the nest for about two months. However, she leaves just before the baby snakes hatch. That's lucky for the babies. The mother is hungry, and snakes are her favorite food!

▲ King cobra eggs

A nest of king cobra eggs

King cobras are the only type of snake that stay with their eggs. Other kinds of snakes just lay their eggs and leave them.

Born to Kill

When a baby snake is ready to hatch, it pokes a hole in its shell and crawls out. Each **hatchling**, already one foot (30 cm) long, is shiny and black with a white belly. It also has bright yellow or white stripes.

As soon as they're born, the hatchlings can flick their tongues, spread their hoods, and growl. They have enough venom to kill a human. In just a few days, the young snakes will be ready to hunt. Even as newborns, they already deserve the name "king."

A king cobra hatchling pushes its way out of its shell.

A hatchling

While a snake's body keeps growing all its life, its skin doesn't grow. As the snake gets bigger, it needs to shed its old skin in order for new skin to form. A young king cobra sheds its skin once a month. An adult sheds three or four times a year.

Fang Facts

- People who are bitten by a king cobra may die within 30 minutes. However, these creatures try to stay away from humans. Fewer than five people die from king cobra bites each year.

- A medicine called antivenin (*an*-tee-VEN-uhn) can save a person who has been bitten by a king cobra. To make antivenin, a very small amount of the snake's venom is injected into a large animal, such as a horse. The animal does not die or get sick. In fact, its body builds up defenses against the venom. Then a small amount of blood is taken from the animal. The antivenin is made from this blood. The medicine can be stored so that it will be ready to inject into a person who needs it.

- The king cobra's venom can also be used to make medicine that can help reduce the pain of people who are sick or injured.

- To get venom from a king cobra, a person holds the snake by the back of its neck. The person then hooks the snake's fangs over the side of a glass. The venom drips into the glass. This is called "milking" a snake.

A king cobra being milked ▶

Glossary

coils
(KOILZ) winds around and around in loops

rain forests
(RAYN FOR-ists) warm places where many trees grow and lots of rain falls

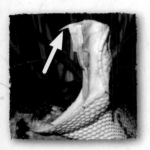

fangs
(FANGZ) long pointy teeth

sacs
(SAKS) parts of an animal's body that are shaped like bags and contain liquid

hatchling
(HACH-ling) a baby snake that has just come out of its egg

strike
(STRIKE) to hit or attack something

prey
(PRAY) animals that are hunted and eaten by other animals

venomous
(VEN-uh-mous) full of poison

Index

Read More

George, Linda. *Cobras.* Mankato, MN: Capstone Press (1998).

Johnson, Sylvia A. *Cobras.* Minneapolis, MN: Lerner Publications Company (2007).

Learn More Online

To learn more about king cobras, visit
www.bearportpublishing.com/Fangs

About the Author

Nancy White has written many science and nature books for children. She lives with her husband and her cat in New York's Hudson River Valley.

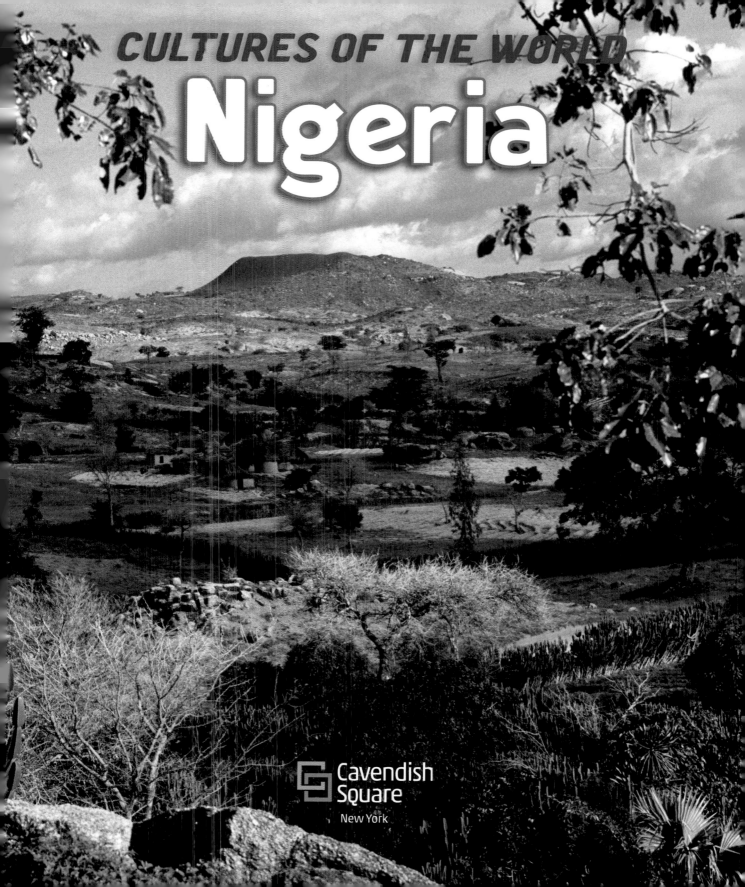

CULTURES OF THE WORLD
Nigeria

Cavendish
Square
New York

Published in 2014 by Cavendish Square Publishing, LLC
303 Park Avenue South, Suite 1247, New York, NY 10010

Third Edition

This publication is published with arrangement with Marshall Cavendish International (Asia) Pte Ltd.

Website: cavendishsq.com

Cultures of the World is a registered trademark of Times Publishing Limited.

This publication represents the opinions and views of the author based on his or her personal experience, knowledge, and research. The information in this book serves as a general guide only. The author and publisher have used their best efforts in preparing this book and disclaim liability rising directly or indirectly from the use and application of this book.

CPSIA Compliance Information: Batch #WW14CSQ

All websites were available and accurate when this book was sent to press.

Library of Congress Cataloging-in-Publication Data
Burbank, Jon.
Nigeria / by Jon Burbank and Josie Elias.
  p. cm. — (Cultures of the world)
Includes index.
ISBN 978-0-76148-014-3 (hardcover) ISBN 978-1-62712-625-0 (paperback) ISBN 978-0-76148-022-8 (ebook)
1. Nigeria — Juvenile literature. I. Burbank, Jon, 1951-. II. Title.
DT515.22 B87 2014
966.9—d23

Writers: Jon Burbank and Josie Elias
Editor: Mindy Pang
Designer: Adithi

PICTURE CREDITS
Audrius Tomonis – www.banknotes.com: 135 • Corbis / Click Photos: 12, 28, 35, 36, 53, 112, 121 • Getty Images: 13, 16, 18, 23, 30, 91, 102, 111, 114 • Inmagine.com / Alamy: 1, 3, 5, 6, 7, 9, 10, 11, 15, 19, 20, 22, 24, 25, 26, 29, 32, 34, 39, 40, 41, 42, 43, 44, 45, 46, 48, 49, 50, 51, 55, 56, 58, 60, 62, 64, 67, 68, 70, 71, 73, 74, 78, 79, 80, 83, 84, 85, 87, 88, 90, 92, 93, 94, 95, 96, 97, 99, 100, 105, 107, 108, 110, 116, 118, 122, 123, 124, 125, 126, 127, 128, 130, 131 • Wikimedia Commons: 98

PRECEDING PAGE
A scenic farming landscape in the city of Jos in Nigeria.

Printed in the United States of America

CONTENTS

NIGERIA TODAY

NIGERIA IS A FEDERAL CONSTITUTIONAL REPUBLIC COMPRISING 36 states and its Federal Capital Territory, Abuja. The country is located in West Africa and is bordered to the north by the Republics of Niger and Chad. It shares borders to the west with the Republic of Benin, while the Republic of Cameroon shares the eastern borders right down to the shores of the Atlantic Ocean, which forms the southern limits of Nigerian Territory. Its coast in the south lies on the Gulf of Guinea on the Atlantic Ocean. The three largest and most influential ethnic groups in Nigeria are the Hausa and Fulani, Igbo, and Yoruba.

In terms of religion Nigeria is roughly split half and half between Muslims in the North and Christians in the South; a very small minority practice traditional religion. Since 2002 there has been a spate of clashes, particularly in the North of the country, between government forces and the Islamists Boko Haram, militant jihadists who seek to establish Islamic law.

Nigeria is the most populous country in Africa, the seventh most populous country in the world, and the most populous country in the world in which the majority of the population is black. Its oil reserves have brought great revenue to the country,

A shrine in the forest of the Osun Sacred Grove in Osogbo.

but sadly, most of the revenue does not filter down to the impoverish population and is lost to corruption.

In 1914, the British formally united the Niger area as the Colony and Protectorate of Nigeria. Administratively, Nigeria remained divided into the northern and southern provinces and Lagos Colony. The people of the South, with more interaction with the British and other Europeans due to the coastal economy, adopted Western education and developed a modern economy more rapidly than in the north. Many of its elite's sons went to Great Britain for education. The regional differences continue to be expressed in Nigeria's political life as well. For instance, northern Nigeria did not outlaw slavery until 1936.

Following World War II, in response to the growth of Nigerian nationalism and demands for independence, successive constitutions legislated by the British government moved Nigeria toward self-government on a representative and increasingly federal basis. By the middle of the 20th century, a great wave for independence was sweeping across Africa. Nigeria became independent in 1960.

Nigeria regained democracy in 1999 when it elected Olusegun Obasanjo, the former military head of state, as the new President of Nigeria ending almost 29 years of military rule (from 1966 until 1999) excluding the short-lived second republic (between 1979 and 1983) by military dictators who seized power in coups d'état and counter-coups during the Nigerian military juntas of 1966 to 1979 and 1983 to 1998. Although the elections which brought Obasanjo to power in 1999 and again in 2003 were condemned as unfree and unfair, Nigeria has shown marked improvements in attempts to tackle government corruption and to hasten development.

Dr. Goodluck Jonathan was declared the winner of Nigeria's 2011 elections. The international media reported the elections as having run smoothly with relatively little violence or voter fraud in contrast to previous elections. However, the elections were followed by communal violence, which left more than 800 people dead.

Nigeria has been undergoing explosive population growth and one of the highest growth and fertility rates in the world. Nigeria is one of eight countries expected to account collectively for half of the world's total population increase from 2005 to 2050. By 2100 the United Nations estimates that the Nigerian population will be about 730 million. In 1950, Nigeria had only 29.8 million people. The current population of Nigeria is 170,123,740.

A baby is weighed at a clinic in Nigeria.

According to current data, one out of every four Africans is Nigerian. Presently, Nigeria is the seventh most populous country in the world, and even conservative estimates conclude that more than 20 percent of the world's black population lives in Nigeria.

Health, healthcare, and general living conditions in Nigeria are poor. Life expectancy is 52 years and just over half the population has access to potable water and appropriate sanitation; the percentage of children under five has gone up rather than down between 1990 and 2003 and the infant mortality rate is 73 deaths for every 1,000 live births. Nigeria suffers from periodic outbreaks of cholera, malaria, and sleeping sickness. It is the only country in Africa to have never eradicated polio, which it periodically exports to other African countries. The state of healthcare in Nigeria has been worsened by a physician shortage as a consequence of severe brain drain. Many Nigerian doctors have migrated to North America and Europe. In 2005, 2,392 Nigerian doctors were practising in the United States alone, and in the United Kingdom, the number was 1,529. Retaining these expensively trained professionals has been identified as an urgent goal.

Education is in a state of neglect. After the 1970s oil boom, tertiary education was improved so that it would reach every subregion of Nigeria. Education is provided free by the government, but the attendance rate for secondary education is only 29 percent. The education system has been described as "dysfunctional" largely because of decaying institutional infrastructure and ill-prepared graduates. Sixty-eight percent of the population is literate, and the rate for men (75.7 percent) is higher than that for women (60.6 percent).

The Delta region has a steadily growing population estimated to be over 30 million people as of 2005, accounting for more than 23 percent of Nigeria's total population. The population density is also among the highest in the world with 265 people per square km. This population is expanding at a rapid 3 percent per year and the oil capital, Port Harcourt, along with other large towns are growing quickly. Poverty and urbanization in Nigeria are on the rise, and official corruption is considered a fact of life. The resultant scenario is one in which there is urbanization but no accompanying economic growth to provide jobs. This has led to a section of the growing populace assisting in destroying the ecosystem that they require to sustain themselves.

The Niger Delta Development Commission (NDDC) was established by President Olusegun Obasanjo with the sole mandate of developing the petroleum-rich Niger-Delta region of southern Nigeria. Since its inauguration, the NDDC has focused on the development of social and physical infrastructures, ecological/environmental remediation, and human development.

On June 26, 2009, the Nigerian Government announced that it would grant amnesty and an unconditional pardon to Militants in the Niger Delta which would last for 60 days beginning on August 6, 2009 and ending on October 4, 2009. Former Nigerian President Umaru Musa Yar'Adua signed the amnesty. Thousands of militants have disarmed under the deal.

Nigeria is home to a substantial network of organized crime, active especially in drug trafficking. Nigerian criminal groups are heavily involved in drug trafficking, shipping heroin from Asian countries to Europe and America, and cocaine from South America to Europe and South Africa. Internationally, Nigeria is infamous for a type of advance fee fraud along with the "Nigerian scam," a form of confidence trick practiced by individuals and criminal syndicates. In 2003, the Nigerian Economic and Financial Crimes Commission (EFCC) was created to combat this and other forms of organized financial crime.

Nigeria has two United Nations Educational, Scientific and Cultural Organization (UNESCO) World Heritage sites—the Sukur Cultural Landscape and the Osun Sacred Grove in Osogbo. The Sukur Cultural Landscape, with the Palace of the Hidi (Chief) on a hill dominating the villages below, the terraced fields and their sacred symbols, and the extensive remains of a former flourishing iron industry, is a remarkably intact physical expression of a society and its spiritual and material culture. It was designated a UNESCO site in 1999 because of its palace, terraced fields, and village, which remain intact. Another site, the dense forest of the Osun Sacred Grove, on the outskirts of the city of Osogbo, is one of the last remnants of primary high forest in southern Nigeria. Regarded as the abode of the goddess of fertility Osun, one of the pantheon of Yoruba gods, the landscape of the grove and its meandering river is dotted with sanctuaries and shrines, sculptures and art works in honor of Osun and other deities. The sacred grove, which is now seen as a symbol of identity for all Yoruba people, is probably the last in Yoruba culture. It testifies to the once widespread practice of establishing sacred groves outside all settlements.

A typical family in Abuja, Nigeria.

The Nigerian government continues to grapple with major crises on both political and economic fronts. On the one hand the government is trying to reform the oil-rich economy, whose revenues have not reached the poor sections of the society due to rampant corruption and poor macroeconomic management. On the other hand longstanding ethnic and religious strife continues to disrupt the day-to-day life of the Nigerians. Despite all these problems the government and law-making agencies are committed to democracy and determined to continue with civilian rule.

GEOGRAPHY

The 1,312-foot (400-meter) Aso Rock is a large outcrop that lies on the outskirts of the capital of Nigeria, Abuja.

AN INDEPENDENT STATE FOR more than 40 years, the Federal Republic of Nigeria is today one of the most dynamic and diverse nations on the African continent. Nigeria is potentially the wealthiest African country, earning export revenue from rubber, oil, tin, and other commodities.

Nigeria's land mass covers an area of 356,669 square miles (923,768 square km), slightly larger than California. Nigeria's natural landscapes range from deserts to tropical rainforests.

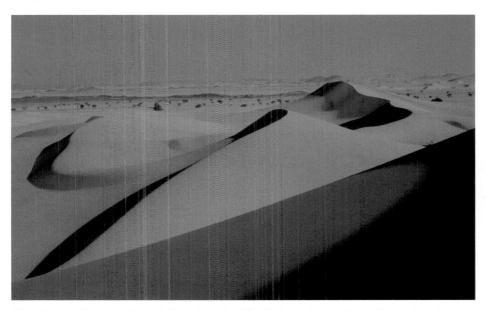

Nigeria's northern plains, while not part of the Sahara desert, have been showing periodic signs of desertification.

Nigeria is facing a population explosion. At its current growth rate, in 25 years Nigeria's population will be 300 million people—the same as the United States' current population—but Nigeria is less than one-tenth the size of the US (900,000 square km versus 9.8 million square km).

Nigeria is the most populous African country, with a population of slightly over 170 million people. Most Nigerians live in rural areas, but increasing numbers of people now see the cities as their means to a better life. Nigerians belong to many ethnic groups and speak different languages, mainly Hausa, Yoruba, and Ibo, or Igbo. English is commonly used and is the official language.

PHYSICAL FEATURES

Nigeria's coastline lies on the Gulf of Guinea in the south. The country shares its western border with Benin and its eastern border with Cameroon. To the north are Niger and Chad. Two rivers divide Nigeria neatly into three. The Niger and Benue rivers meet in the center of the country before flowing south to the Niger Delta.

The Niger Delta, the delta of the Niger River in Nigeria, is a densely populated region sometimes called the "Oil Rivers" because it was once a major producer of palm oil. The area was the British Oil Rivers Protectorate

Plenty of oil fields are found in the Niger Delta near Escravos. Many energy companies have their main base and storage facilities in this area.

from 1885 until 1893, when it was expanded and became the Niger Coast Protectorate. The Niger Delta, as now defined officially by the Nigerian government, extends over about 27,027 square miles (70,000 square km) and makes up 7.5 percent of Nigeria's land mass. Inside it, the Niger River spreads into hundreds of shifting channels. The delta is the result of thousands of tons of soil being washed down by the river over hundreds of years. Vast crude oil and natural gas reserves have been discovered in the delta.

The channels in the delta are shallow and difficult to navigate, apart from the Escravos River. Big seafaring ships regularly navigate the Escravos, which provides access to the ports of Burutu, Koko, Sapele, and Warri.

Nigeria's coastline is sheltered from the open sea by a narrow belt of coastal swamps, lagoons, and creeks. North of the coast, the mangrove swamps give way to tropical rainforests, and the terrain gets drier farther toward the north as the rainforests give way to savanna and finally to the desolation of the desert in the extreme north.

Mangrove swamps in Bonny Island. The southerly portion of Nigeria's coastal plains is defined as salt water swamps, often called mangrove swamps, because of the large number of mangroves in the area.

CLIMATE

Nigeria's climate is largely tropical. There are rainy and dry seasons, depending on the movements of two air masses: a dry air mass over the

Sahara Desert to the north and a moist air mass over the South Atlantic. The air masses meet over Nigeria and create bands of weather that move as the year progresses.

Between November and March, the dry air mass dominates the whole country, bringing drought to northern Nigeria. At this time the south has little rainfall. The point where the two air masses meet moves northward in April, and the south then experiences heavy tropical rainstorms. It becomes very humid and the sky is almost continually overcast. In the north the rains are also heavy.

After August the weather reverses so that by December the south is again experiencing light rain and the north drought. A wind called *harmattan* (har-mat-TAN) blows dust clouds from the Sahara Desert to northern Nigeria and lowers temperatures.

RIVERS

While many neighboring nations suffer from drought every year, Nigeria enjoys a constant supply of water from two major river systems. The rivers also serve as channels of transportation.

The **Benue River** is almost entirely navigable during the summer months. It is an important transportation route in the regions through which it flows.

THE SIGHTS AND SOUNDS OF THE NIGERIAN RAINFOREST

The Nigerian rainforest is home to towering trees, from hardwoods to bamboo and palm. Hardwoods such as iroko, sapele, and obeche are used in making furniture and are important to the Nigerian economy. Flame-of-the-forest trees can be identified by their striking red flowers. Small white orchids may grow from the branches of flame-of-the-forest trees.

High up in the Nigerian rainforest canopy, monkeys chatter and hornbills caw. On the forest floor, dead logs offer shelter to industrious insects and slithering snakes, and the air is filled with the incessant noise of cicadas and crickets.

Small animals, notably tiny antelope, thrive in the Nigerian rain forest. However, the more dangerous creatures that once threatened explorers, such as the famous Scottish Mungo Park (1771—1806), have become elusive.

Starting in the Fouta Djallon highlands of Guinea, the 2,600-mile (4,184-km) Niger, one of the world's longest rivers, flows north through Mali and then curves south through Niger and Nigeria toward the Gulf of Guinea. Along its course, the river is tapped for irrigation and to produce electricity. In Nigeria, the Kainji dam and reservoir provide water from the Niger River to irrigate farmland and generate hydroelectric power.

Once the Benue joins the Niger in central Nigeria, the river is navigable. Before an adequate road system was built in the area, the river was an important route for boats. The Niger and Benue are each about a mile (1.6 km) wide where they meet and form a large body of water that resembles a lake dotted with sandbanks and islands.

Farther south, the Niger flows through sandstone cliffs 150 feet (45.7 m) high and becomes deeper and more rapid. Still farther downstream, the river flows slowly over relatively flat land. It floods regularly during the rainy season and causes substantial damage, often because trees caught in the flood smash into buildings or fences on the riverbank.

The Benue, the largest tributary of the Niger, is fed by many smaller rivers originating in the highlands of the Jos Plateau. Many of these rivers have been dammed to create a steady water supply for people living in the surrounding areas and a source of hydroelectric power for the tin mines of the Jos Plateau.

Another important Nigerian river is the Cross in the southeast. Before the development of road and rail, the river was the main thoroughfare of the Cross River state and its capital city, Calabar (cal-ah-BAR), was a focal point for trade.

THE RAINFOREST

A tropical rainforest belt 170 miles (274 km) wide lay across southern Nigeria before people settled there. The forest supported a large animal community including buffalo, bushbucks, elephants, leopards, and wild boar. Most of that forest cover has been cleared to make space for agriculture and to harvest hardwood timber for industry and export. Only a fraction of the original rain forest remains, supporting a tiny number of the animals that once lived there.

What is left of the Nigerian rainforest is very similar in content and organization to other rainforests in South America and Asia. The density and type of vegetation vary with altitude. The topmost layer of the forest

View from the canopy layer of a rainforest in Nigeria.

consists of the foliage of the tallest trees. The layer below the canopy is made up of the leaves of trees with buttressed roots. The second layer is also often characterized by woody climbing plants. At ground level, there is a thin layer of bush, with herbs carpeting the ground. The flora of the tropical rainforest is evergreen.

THE SAVANNA

Savanna covers central Nigeria, an arid part of the country. Dry weather persists for months in the region, and fires are a frequent possibility. Bush fires may be accidental or deliberate. In the latter case, farmers start fires in the savanna to clear the land for their own use.

The savanna typically consists of high grasses interspersed with trees and smaller shrubs. Frequent fires have eliminated the more delicate plants, and trees have disappeared due to either bush fires or the work of firewood collectors.

THE NORTHERN PLAINS

The northern plains of Nigeria cover a large area, beginning in the Jos Plateau. Before the plains were cultivated, they were covered by short grasses and hardy, thorny trees, such as acacia. The plains receive no rain for half the year, and the rivers dry up completely. Some people believe that eventually the Sahara Desert will extend to cover the northernmost parts of Nigeria's northern plains.

The Jos Plateau covers 3,000 square miles (7,770 square km) and is bounded by 3,200 feet (975 m) cliffs around much of its circumference.

A local canoes to travel from Nigeria to Lake Bol, part of Lake Chad. In less than 30 years, Lake Chad has shrunk to a third of its original size. People who still live around the basin are looking at grounded boats and barren land which was once under water.

THE JOS PLATEAU

The Jos Plateau is located almost in the center of Nigeria. It rises 4,200 feet (1,280 m) above the surrounding plains, and at the edges it drops suddenly and sharply to the plains below.

The weather on the plateau is distinctly cooler and wetter than the weather in the plains. The plateau is densely populated, and cash crops are farmed there, including the Irish potato.

The Jos Plateau has been extensively mined for tin, and abandoned mines have been used for irrigation projects using the shadoof.

KAINJI DAM

Completed in 1968, the damming of the Niger at Kainji resulted in the creation of a lake 90 miles (145 km) long and up to 17 miles (27 km) wide. The 500 square-mile (1,295 square-km) lake required the resettlement of 42,000 people. To replace their homes, 117 new villages and two new towns were built in a modern architectural style.

The Kainji Dam generates hydroelectric power and has the potential to support large-scale irrigation projects. It was shut down on March 16, 2012 because of water leakages. Repairs to four out of the five pumping stations were completed on March 26, 2012, and the CEO claimed that 100 megawatts (MW) would be generated by the dam once it was fully repaired.

LAKE CHAD

Nigeria shares Lake Chad, located in the extreme north, with Cameroon, Chad, and Niger. The remains of an inland sea, the very shallow lake shrinks to half its size during the dry season. It provides fish and some minerals, as well as water for cattle that graze on its shores. Most of the lake's shore in Nigeria has not yet been exploited agriculturally, and it remains marshy, unused land.

An aerial view
of Lagos.

MANGROVES

The Nigerian coastline is characterized by swamps and lagoons, with lianas and palms that make it difficult for people to navigate and move around. Where the swampy land comes into contact with the sea, there are mangrove forests. The roots of the mangrove trees are like stilts, supporting the plant above the surface of the water while anchoring it to the soil.

Mangroves grow in salty water. Their stilt roots also encourage the growth of marine creatures such as oysters and shrimp. The seeds of the mangrove germinate while still inside the pod on the tree, and put down aerial roots into the water.

MAJOR CITIES

LAGOS Lagos was the capital city of Nigeria until 1991, and it remains the commercial, industrial, and cultural hub of the country. Built on a series of islands in a lagoon, Lagos is sheltered from the enormous waves of the Atlantic Ocean by a series of smaller islands and sandbanks that are connected by bridges. A railway was constructed in the early 20th century to provide trade links with the interior.

Lagos island, the original site of the city, houses government offices, major department stores, and office blocks. Industry has developed around the railway and harbor, and many people commute from the suburbs of Lagos into the city center every day.

Officially, the population of Lagos was last recorded at 10.203 million. Lagos is the second fastest growing city in Africa and the seventh fastest in the world.

CREATING A NEW CITY—ABUJA

The plan for Abuja was to create a new city unlike any in Nigeria—fully equipped with the necessary infrastructure before the arrival of residents and workers. Abuja would be within the Federal Capital Territory, in the heart of Nigeria.

Today, Abuja has a population of 1.86 million. It occupies an area of around 3,089 square miles (8,000 square km) and is divided into two zones: one for civil and government buildings such as embassies, the National Assembly, and the offices of ministers; and the other for homes, shops, and factories. Abuja has a university and

an international airport and is the location for the head offices of many national and international banks. The capital city has an orderly road network, and there are plans for a metro system. Surrounding the city is a large area of agricultural land that supports the city's food needs and provides a green area for rest and relaxation.

Lagos became overpopulated in the 1960s and 1970s, and its infrastructure began to crumble under the pressure. A decision was made in 1976 to move the capital to a more central location. After more than a decade of planning and development, the new city of Abuja and the Federal Capital Territory were built, and Lagos lost its official status as capital of Nigeria in 1991.

IBADAN Ibadan spreads over 16 square miles (41 square km) of hilly terrain. During the civil war in 1829 Ibadan was a walled city used in military defense. By 1851 most of the inhabitants of Ibadan were commuting daily to their farms in the surrounding countryside. The population of the city still consists mainly of commuting farmers. Under the British, Ibadan was the capital of western Nigeria.

Different ethnic groups live in separate districts in Ibadan. Outsiders, such as the Hausa-Fulani, or settlers from other continents, such as the Europeans or Lebanese, live in designated areas within the town. In Ibadan, members of an extended family live close to one another and share farmland. Town life revolves around the markets, which serve wholesalers in the morning, housewives in the afternoon, and families looking for a meal in the evening.

Ibadan is connected to the former capital city of Lagos by rail and is Nigeria's third-largest city, after Lagos and Kano. It is congested and overcrowded, as all Nigerian cities tend to be, but it throbs with life. The city has a university and parks, and the surrounding farms and factories produce furniture, handicrafts, and cotton.

KADUNA Built in 1913, Kaduna was once the capital city of northern Nigeria. It is typical of cities in the northern states, with broad avenues and planned areas for commercial and government buildings, and staff quarters. Kaduna also has an industrial section and a railroad depot conveniently located close to the city center, and the city is well-known for its universities, training colleges, and other educational institutions. Many Kaduna residents are connected with the national armed forces.

Centered in the cotton-growing area of Nigeria, Kaduna also has a car assembly plant, textile factories, and an oil refinery connected by pipeline to oil fields in the Niger Delta.

INTERNET LINKS

www.motherlandnigeria.com/geography.html

A comprehensive page on the geography of Nigeria, complete with links to each city's website.

www.mongabay.com/reference/new_profiles/183ng.html

Concise facts about Nigeria's geography.

http://kids.yahoo.com/reference/world-factbook/country/ni--Nigeria

Interesting facts on Nigeria in bite-sized pieces.

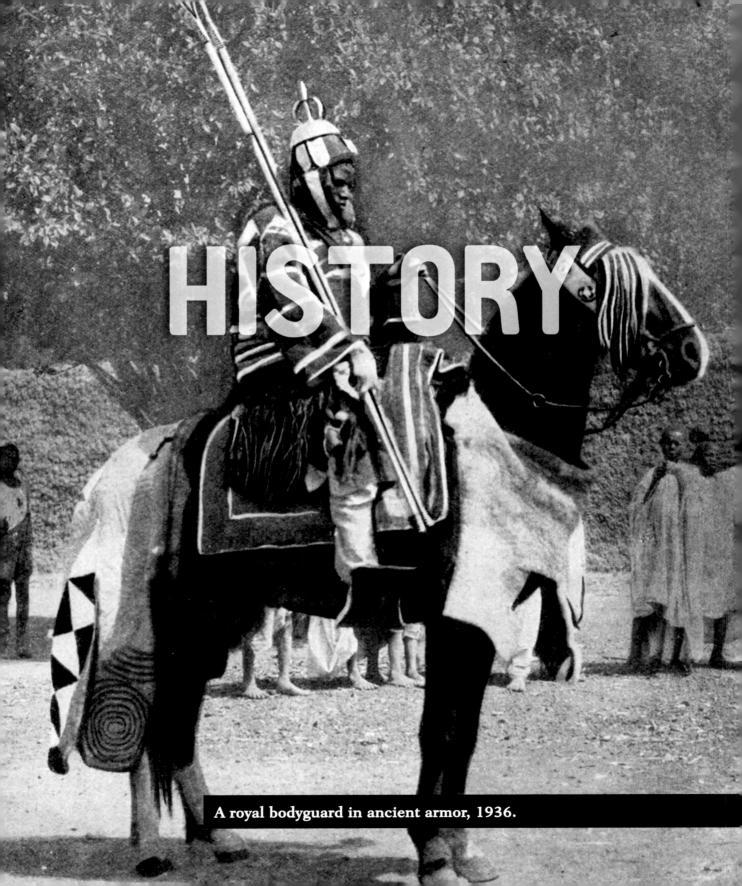

A royal bodyguard in ancient armor, 1936.

U NTIL THE 19TH CENTURY, the nation known today as Nigeria was a patchwork of small ethnic groups. Conflicts occurred within territories such as the Yoruba lands, with one group taking slaves from another.

Groups in the south tended to organize without a form of government, while in the north Islamic kingdoms were born out of a series of jihads, or holy wars.

The lack of a central government in the region seemed to suit the Europeans, who found it easy to exploit the region. But after slavery was abolished, some Europeans began to settle in the area and needed a system of government to protect themselves.

A painting of the Market in Sokoto in 1853. Spanish and Portuguese explorers were the first Europeans to begin trade in Nigeria in the 16th century. They began trading goods with the people of the coast but soon entered the African slave trade.

2

The Federation of Nigeria was granted full independence on October 1, 1960.

Ancient sites in the Jos Plateau region contain clues about life in Nigeria between the fifth and third centuries B.C. People then had learned how to make iron tools to clear the ground and till the soil for crop cultivation. They also made iron weapons. Some of the Nok sculptures and pottery show figures carrying iron axes.

The terracotta statues of the ancient Nok culture of Nigeria were excavated in the 1990s in the Jos Plateau region. Many of them are models of human heads or animals at least 1,500 years old. The sculptures shed light on the sophistication and lifestyle of the Nok people.

Models of cattle that have been discovered show the breed that the Nok domesticated. The models had no humps like those of cattle found in Nigeria today.

Many of the Nok sculptures also show evidence of having been copied from wood carvings.

At the turn of the 20th century the British created a protectorate, bringing together much of the Nigeria of today, although geographical and social barriers still divided the north from the east and the west.

THE PRE-COLONIAL NORTH

The first example of a modern state in Nigeria was the Kanem-Bornu kingdom, which made Borno, in the northeast of what is today Nigeria, its political center. Established by the 13th century, the Kanem-Borno kingdom consisted of city-states, which collected taxes to support the kingdom's

A view of Kano city in the 1860s.

armies, in particular cavalry regiments. The kingdom adopted Islam in the 11th century.

West of Borno, some Hausa states became part of the Songhai Empire in the 1400s and 1500s. After the empire collapsed, the Islamic caliphates of Hausaland and Sokoto flourished but later became corrupt and lost many of their Islamic values.

A nomadic Islamic people, the Fulani, gained influence and brought about a religious revival. Accusing the leaders of abusing their power, collecting taxes illegally, and practicing polytheism, the Fulani leader Usman dan Fodio launched a jihad against the Hausa overlords in 1804. Similar wars prevailed all over the region, establishing a Fulani empire, with Sokoto as its center.

THE SOUTHERN STATES

The history of the southern states is clouded in myth and legend. Study of archaeological sites shows that the eastern and western halves of the south followed different patterns of civilization.

In the east, communities tended to be stateless. Settlements were small and far apart. Well into the 20th century, leaders tended to be people who had shown themselves worthy of respect. There were no formal elections, only a consensus that a particular person had the right to determine the village's future.

In the west, Ife (EE-fay) was an established Yoruba cultural center by the 11th century. Two powerful states arose from the western civilization: Benin and Oyo.

In the 12th century Benin was the capital of a state that extended from the Niger to Lagos. It traded with Europeans and was visited by the Portuguese explorer João Afonso d'Aveiro in 1486. Trade began with products such as pepper but quickly expanded to include slaves and initiated the boom years of the slave industry.

Oyo, the other major state to evolve from Ife, extended its authority westward during the 1700s into what is today the Republic of Benin. The Oyo armies were cavalry-based, operating outside the rainforest belt where there was less threat to livestock from tsetse flies.

THE 19TH CENTURY

Just about the time that the Fulani were launching their holy wars in northern Nigeria, the British decided that slavery was wrong and ceased trade with the slave dealers who had for many years benefited from a lucrative relationship with the British.

The British ban had little effect on the slave trade. The Yoruba and Fulani wars generated large numbers of slaves. The trade simply moved westward,

THE FULANI STATES

The Fulani caliphs constructed a complex social structure in the local communities. They nominated people to administer the communities. Each community had a tax collector who collected taxes on land and on farm produce. Each handicraft guild had a leader who collected taxes from members and sent the revenues to the state capital. The caliphs used the revenues to help the poor, build mosques, and provide utilities.

and slave dealers learned to evade the British navy. As a consequence, British forces attacked and burned Lagos in 1851 and occupied the city in 1861.

British influence increased, and by 1884 Britain had established a monopoly on the legitimate commodity of the area—palm oil. British missionaries spread throughout southern Nigeria, bringing education to those who would later constitute the administrative class of another stronghold of the British Empire.

For the most part, Britain kept out of internal wars, except when it affected trade. But in 1884 Britain claimed Nigeria. Yorubaland, still plagued by internal wars, was brought under control by treaty. Benin, which was a slaving stronghold, was approached in 1897 by a British trading mission, but its troops massacred the British force.

In reprisal, the British sent a larger and more aggressive force against Benin, and the city was razed. They encroached into Fulani territory but were relatively unsuccessful until they systematically attacked the area using superior firepower. In 1903 Sokoto surrendered to the British, and its sultan fled.

The British were few in number and vulnerable to diseases such as smallpox, diphtheria, malaria, and leprosy. They designated local rulers as their representatives to collect taxes and administer their areas. The emirs lost their power and were replaced by the British governor. The *zakat* (za-KAT) tax, which had funded education and provided for the needs of the poor and infirm, was abolished. Nothing replaced it to continue providing such services.

The British restricted missionary activity and the north became underdeveloped, with education denied to its children. Schools were closed

The slave trade powered the economy of settlements along the coast of Nigeria. Small fishing villages became city-states within a few decades. The Aro subgroup of the Ibo people, who lived mainly in the southeast, became the area's procurers of slaves, taking people from the interior to the coast and exchanging them for salt, cloth, metals, and tools. The process remained in the hands of African dealers until the slaves boarded the European ships.

A child presents a bouquet to Queen Elizabeth of England during her visit to Nigeria in February 1956 to inaugurate the Federal Court in Lagos.

and textbook requests rejected. By 1914 the Sokoto area, with a population of 1.4 million, had only 19 elementary schools. The effects of the British policy were far-reaching, and for a long time the north was politically disadvantaged.

By the end of World War II, an adequate number of Nigerians had become well-traveled and educated enough to realize that Nigeria had a right to self-government. The British had effectively kept the various parts of the country isolated politically and, in educating the south but not the north, had created jealousy and bitterness that have dogged attempts to establish democracy since Britain withdrew.

In 1946 a new constitution was established giving power to the three regions—north, west, and east—but maintaining British control of the central government. Newer versions in 1951 and 1954 strengthened regional powers against those of the central government.

THE BRITISH PROTECTORATE

When the southern and northern regions were amalgamated into one protectorate in 1914, they had little in common apart from their British rulers. Over the next 40 years, the British protectorate's economy expanded tremendously, particularly in exports.

The companies that controlled and profited from exports were all British. Cocoa, cotton, hardwoods, palm oil, peanuts, and tin provided British companies with huge profits.

A railroad system was established that connected Port Harcourt and Lagos with production areas in the north, and a road network linked the major ports with the east.

INDEPENDENCE DAY

The years preceding Nigeria's independence saw the establishment of three major political parties based on regional loyalties. Denied education during the British years, the north was economically weaker than the south and less able to contribute to the central government.

Nigeria became an independent republic on October 1, 1963, with a British-style constitution dating from 1960. The government could not handle the strain caused by conflicting national and regional interests. In addition, corruption charges led to treason trials and then general strikes and attempted coups, setting a pattern that has come to characterize present-day Nigeria.

The federal system of government was abandoned in 1966 by General Johnson T. U. Aguiyi-Ironsi, an Ibo, who was declared the temporary head of state. He tried to deal with regionalism by setting up a strong central government. In July that year, he was ousted and killed, and a new supreme commander, General Yakubu Gowon, came to power.

Yakubu Gowon was the head of the state of Nigeria from 1966 to 1975.

THE BIAFRAN WAR

Interregional rivalry led to the mass murder of the Ibo, who held many government positions. The massacres fueled plans for secession in the east, where the Ibo were dominant. As Ibo in the north and south moved east, Gowon declared 12 states to reduce eastern power. Four days later, the east seceded as the independent Republic of Biafra.

The Nigerian government received the backing of the West, and few African states recognized Biafran independence; they too consisted of poorly meshed ethnic groups and could suffer the same fate if powerful areas seceded. Biafra held out for 30 months. Its people were driven east into forest and swampland, and thousands died of starvation.

The slaves who were transported from West Africa to the West Indies and the United States were the ancestors of most present-day African-Americans.

POST-CIVIL WAR NIGERIA

Gowon's regime post-civil war focused on unifying the country. Oil revenues spiraled upward owing to the oil price boom of the 1970s. A massive development plan was underway when the third coup since independence took place and Gowon was replaced by the reformist Brigadier Murtala Muhammad. A supreme military council was formed, and many high-ranking officers and heads of service were retired.

The stage seemed set for progress when a counter-coup occurred, killing Muhammad. The coup was unsuccessful. Within a month, 32 people involved in the coup were publicly executed. The new government embarked on reforms funded by oil revenues, and a U.S.-style democracy was chosen. In 1979 Nigeria returned to civilian rule, led by the northerner Shehu Shagari.

Four years later, military power resumed, led by Major General Muhammad Buhari. He was killed in a 1985 coup that brought General Ibrahim Babangida to power. After several postponements, elections in May 1992 put the Social Democratic Party (SDP) in power. Babangida, citing irregularities, nullified the elections and retained power.

Elections were held again in June 1993. Moshood Abiola, a Muslim Yoruba leader of the SDP, won. However, the election was ruled invalid, and military rule continued. General Babingida resigned under pressure in August 1993, and General Sani Abacha, the secretary of defense under Babangida, became the new military ruler of Nigeria.

That year General Sani Abacha seized power. He banned political institutions and labor unions, arrested or murdered political dissidents, and in 1995 executed Ken Saro-Wiwa and eight other human rights activists. Nigeria was suspended from the British Commonwealth, and when Abacha died in 1998, he was replaced by a calmer military ruler, General Abdulsalam Abubakar, who released political prisoners and began preparations to return Nigeria to democratic rule.

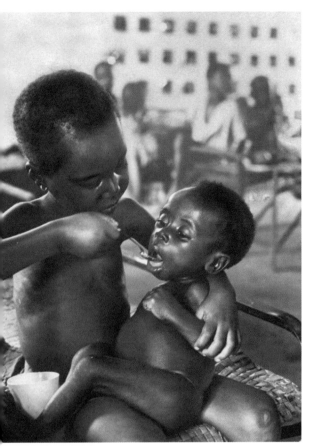

A hungry child feeds another. The real victims of the civil war, thousands of starving and malnourished Biafran children were seeking help from refugee centers in 1968.

In 1999 Olusegun Obasanjo, a former military ruler who was later imprisoned for opposing military rule, was elected president. His government had to deal with problems such as corruption in the government and military, and ethnic and religious divisions. The latter have claimed and continue to claim thousands of lives.

The emergence of democracy in Nigeria on May 1999 ended 15 years of consecutive military rule. Olusegun Obasanjo inherited a country suffering economic stagnation and the deterioration of most democratic institutions. The President retired hundreds of military officers holding political positions, established a panel to investigate human rights violations, released scores of persons held without charge, and rescinded numerous questionable licenses and contracts left by the previous regimes. The government also moved to recover millions of dollars in funds secreted to overseas accounts.

Most civil society leaders and Nigerians witnessed marked improvements in human rights and freedom of the press under Obasanjo, who was reelected in 2003. In the 2007 general elections, Umaru Yar'Adua and Goodluck Jonathan, both of the People's Democratic Party (PDP), were elected President and Vice President respectively. Yar'Adua's presidency was fraught with uncertainty as media reports said he suffered from kidney and heart disease. In November 2009, he fell ill and was flown out of the country to Saudi Arabia for medical attention. In February 2010, Goodluck Jonathan began serving as acting President in the absence of Yar'Adua. Goodluck Jonathan called for new elections and stood for reelection in April 2011. He won and is currently the president of Nigeria.

In 1985 Babangida annulled the 1979 constitution and formed the Armed Forces Ruling Council (AFRC) as the new government. In 1992, after denying the SDP their election success, he renamed his government the National Defense and Security Council.

INTERNET LINKS

www.timeforkids.com/destination/nigeria/history-timeline
Cool interactive timeline on the history of Nigeria for kids.

www.state.gov/r/pa/ei/bgn/2836.htm#history
An informative, up-to-date website on the history of Nigeria.

www.ng.total.com/01_about_nigeria/0103_history.htm
A comprehensive website on the history of Nigeria.

GOVERNMENT

Stoic army soldiers lining up at a government parade.

3

NIGERIAN HISTORY REVEALS one of its major problems—establishing the type of government that the country needs. Before the Europeans came, there was no country called Nigeria. The land was divided into three regions, each torn by internal differences. In 1914 the British brought the regions together under one administrative umbrella, but they kept the three regions isolated from one another.

As such, the republic that Nigeria's new government inherited in 1963 was difficult to govern due not only to ethnic diversity but also to dissension and religious rivalry.

ETHNIC CONFLICT

Before the British brought railroads and economic progress to Nigeria, the diverse practices of the various regions and peoples generated conflicts that prevented the formation of a stable community.

For example, slavery was widespread in Nigeria before the European incursions into Africa. Groups took slaves from among their own people as well as from rivals. Human sacrifice and cannibalism also existed in parts of Nigeria.

Signs remain of the ethnic conflicts that marked precolonial life in Nigeria. In many cities, the walls that once protected the citizens from attack by their neighbors still stand.

CONSTITUTIONAL HISTORY

After the Richards Constitution of 1946 failed, the British passed the Macpherson Constitution of 1951. Although it took into account views from the local level, it also failed. The constitution of 1951 gave limited legislative power to the regions but encouraged representatives in the national government to act in favor of their own regions.

Subsequent efforts to remake Nigeria's constitution, including postindependence ones, consistently fell short of the needs and expectations of the citizenry and government. In 1966 alone, there were two military coups—one by southern generals, one by generals from the northern region. They replaced the structure of the civilian government with a supreme military council. Soldiers filled all top government and civil positions, and state governors were also soldiers.

Although a brutal system of government, military rule controlled corruption and gave national issues priority over local ones. In 1976 the military government reorganized Nigeria into 19 states in an attempt to dissipate regional power. In 1987 two new states were established, followed

The Emir of Kano, his Royal Highness Alhaji Dr Ado Bayero, holds court at his palace.

by another nine in 1991, bringing the total to 30. The latest change, in 1996, resulted in the present number of 36 states.

RETURN TO DEMOCRACY In 1979 Nigeria gave democracy another chance. The constitution was safeguarded to prevent any region from determining national policy. The president was elected to a term of four years and needed a majority in at least 13 of the 19 states then. The Senate and House of Representatives were directly elected for four-year terms. A system of checks and balances, much like that of the United States, with two houses and the presidency, was installed.

Major General Muhammadu Buhari, dictator of Nigeria, following a successful coup d'état against Shehu Shagari in 1983. He was himself overthrown in a coup in 1985.

Within each state in Nigeria, a governor was elected for a four-year term, and house-of-assembly members also served four-year terms. The regional government developed state economy, health, and education. The state also managed all direct taxes, including income tax. As in the United States, national laws took precedence over state laws.

The Nigerian president and senate had little power. The House of Representatives had the most power and was elected on a population basis. So the most densely populated areas of the country dominated the government.

There were no national political parties, only local leaders with the interests of their own state at heart. Northerners held 167 of the 312 seats and consequently dominated parliament. Government jobs were given out unfairly, and national laws that served regional interests were passed. Each region had its own government, modeled on the national one, and its own civil service.

Nigeria's second try at civilian rule coincided with enormous oil-generated revenues. Political corruption led to the diversion of the oil revenues into private citizens' hands and eventually led to the bloodless coup of 1983.

Nigeria has since seen a succession of military rulers, with short democratic intervals. Nigeria has an elected president and a bicameral National Assembly in which three political parties are represented.

POLITICAL CORRUPTION

Under military rule, civil courts had no jurisdiction over matters such as corruption, which was—and some say still is—rife in Nigeria. In the interim period between military and civilian rule in 1999, huge amounts of the national reserves were set aside for oil exploration, building, and other projects all in the hands of the outgoing military rulers who were given the contracts for the work uncontested. A little of that money has been handed back to the state since democracy was reestablished. There are now controls in place to prevent such corruption.

In 2003, for the first time in 43 years of independence, a civilian administration was reelected. There were reports by foreign observers of corruption at the ballot stations, such as tampered ballot boxes, but the elections passed with little rioting, and international observers generally accepted the process as fair. However, during the next presidential elections held in 2007 human rights groups accused the ruling party and electoral officials of fraud and violence that marred the polling process in some areas.

More than 73 million eligible voters in the most populous African nation will vote at
120,000 polling stations across the country for their next president.

HUMAN RIGHTS

Nigeria has a poor human rights record. Closed-door trials, detention without charge, and executions and floggings were common in the 1980s. Opposition political leaders and human rights activists were assassinated or executed in the 1990s. States in the north that follow Islamic law deal out harsh sentences such as death by stoning for actions not considered a crime in most parts of the world, such as conceiving a child out of wedlock.

Gender equality does not exist in Nigeria. Women lose many rights after marriage. Religious tolerance is eroding. An attempt in 2002 to stage the Miss World contest in Abuja led to religious and ethnic riots that killed hundreds.

While some areas of human rights have suffered badly, others have slowly improved. For example, there are independent daily newspapers published in the country, when in 1994 all except government-controlled newspapers were banned.

The 2011 presidential elections were praised by the international media as the fairest in Nigeria's history as compared to the previous elections. However, widespread post-election violence was reported, which left more than 800 people dead.

POLITICS AND POLITICAL PARTIES

Before the 1966 coups, three parties roughly represented the northern, eastern, and western regions. After the second attempt at democracy in 1979, laws were passed insisting that parties have a national basis. That worked quite successfully, with all parties rejecting regionalism.

In 1983 the new military government banned all political parties. Two parties formed in 1989, the Social Democratic Party (SDP) and the National Republican Convention (NRC), still function but do not hold office.

With the reintroduction of democracy in 1999, three major parties dominated Nigerian politics. The All Nigeria People's Party (ANPP), the Alliance for Democracy (AD), and the ruling People's Democratic Party (PDP) represented national rather than regional or ethnic interests.

In addition, many smaller groups draw support from an ethnic or religious group or region. For example, the Odua People's Congress in the southwest

Nigeria's courts have operated independently of the government since 1999. The president appoints Supreme Court judges, while the federal government appoints federal court appeal judges.

The electoral register in 2003, based on the 1991 census, counted 60 million eligible voters. Despite the availability of 70 million registration forms thousands of people claimed that they could not register. International observers were called in to look out for occurrences of ballot rigging and other fraud. However, large number of Nigerian citizens in the southeast boycotted the elections. Observers from the European Union reported cases of police officers stuffing ballot boxes with forged votes.

The 2007 elections can be regarded as the worst in Nigeria's post-independence history. There were reports of rampant malpractices, such as failures in late delivery of voting materials, delay in commencement of polls in most states, falsification of votes, and so on.

During the 2011 presidential polls 73 million registered voters were expected to cast their vote. The run-up to the elections was marred by ethnic violence due to which the elections were postponed by a week.

of the country claims to represent the interests of the Yoruba people and strongly favors greater regional power for the area.

Political groups in the north are based on religious affiliation, with groups in the delta region further splintered along ethnic lines. Nigeria faces a serious problem in bringing all these diverse interests together.

Nigeria's other political parties include the United Nigeria People's Party, the Party for Social Democracy, and the Green Party of Nigeria.

THE PRESENT

Nigeria in the 21st century is enjoying a period of stable democratic government after almost half a century of independence and several switches between military and civilian rule. There is freedom of the press, and citizens have the right to form political parties. The latter, however, has resulted in what might be the next major obstacle to stable government in Nigeria.

As many as 30 small parties exist, each representing an ethnic or religious group in a particular region. The groups want either greater representation in the state government or greater control over their own region.

The president is elected by universal suffrage. He/she is both the chief of state and head of government and heads the Federal Executive Council, or cabinet.

The adoption of Islamic law in the northern states has caused friction between Muslims and Christians, resulting in riots and murders. States in the north also want more control in the national government in order to bring more of the southern oil revenues under their control. Pipelines in the delta area have been sabotaged and oil companies forced out of the region. The Ibo, who once declared the east an independent state, claim that they have been shut out of the government.

The Federal Secretariat building in Abuja.

The Odua People's Congress (OPC) promotes Yoruba interests and advocates either Yoruba autonomy in the southwest of Nigeria or an independent Yoruba republic. The Arewa Peoples Congress (APC), a radical group in the north, was formed in opposition to the OPC. The APC protects the interests of northern ethnic groups in Nigeria.

INTERNET LINKS

www.commonwealth-of-nations.org/Nigeria/Government/Government_Ministries

Links to the websites of all the government ministries in Nigeria.

www.commonwealth-of-nations.org/Nigeria/Government/Government_Ministries

All the political news of Nigeria in one website.

www.bribenigeria.com/

A website dedicated to fighting corruption in Nigeria by having people post stories of their having to fight corruption on a daily basis in Nigeria.

ECONOMY

Nigeria is the twelfth-largest producer of petroleum in the world and the eighth-largest exporter. They also have the tenth-largest proven reserves.

4

NIGERIA IS AN EMERGING market economy. It is ranked 31st in the world in terms of Gross Domestic Product (GDP) as of 2012, and its manufacturing sector is the third-largest on the continent, producing a large proportion of goods and services for the West African region.

Previously hindered by years of mismanagement, economic reforms of the past decade have put Nigeria back on track towards achieving

The headquarters of the Central Bank of Nigeria in Abuja.

its full economic potential. Nigerian GDP more than tripled from $112.3 billion in 2005 to $455.5 billion in 2012, although estimates of the size of the informal sector (which is not included in official figures) put the actual numbers closer to $520 billion. Correspondingly, the GDP per person doubled from $1,200 per person in 2005 to an estimated $2,800 per person in 2012 (again, with the inclusion of the informal sector, it is estimated that GDP per capita hovers around $3,500 per person).

BATTLE AGAINST CORRUPTION

Former President Olusegun Obasanjo's campaign against corruption, which includes the arrest of officials accused of misdeeds and recovering stolen funds, has won praise from the World Bank. In September 2005, Nigeria, with the assistance of the World Bank, began to recover US$458 million of illicit funds that had been deposited in Swiss banks by the late military dictator Sani Abacha, who ruled Nigeria from 1993 to 1998. However, while broad-based progress has been slow, these efforts have begun to become evident in international surveys of corruption. As a matter of fact, Nigeria's anti-corruption ranking has consistently improved.

An employee at the Peugeot Automobile Factory in Kaduna. Large market and relatively affordable options have made Nigerian automobile sales retain its lucrative status, despite the global economic recession.

AGRICULTURE

About 39 percent of Nigerians live off the land, mostly as subsistence farmers who sell some cash crops to supplement their income. When the oil boom led to reduced crop output, it became easier and cheaper to import food staples such as sugar and corn than to increase agricultural investment to ensure long-term self-sufficiency.

Palm oil became Nigeria's most important export after the slave trade was abolished in the late 19th century. The British set up a colony to handle the trade at Lagos. Today, Nigeria's palm tree belt stretches from Calabar in

Nigeria's main peanut-producing areas are located around Kano in the north, where the climate is similar to that in California. Peanut oil is extracted by crushing, heating, and pressing the kernels. It is used for cooking and to manufacture margarine. Peanut oil is replacing palm oil in Nigeria's domestic economy.

the east to Ibadan in the west. Palm oil is generally harvested from trees in the wild. The oil is pressed from the palm fruit, which grows in football-sized bunches on trees about 30 feet (9 m) tall.

Nigeria's rubber is similarly tapped from trees in the wild. The British exported the rubber in its raw state. Today, Nigeria processes much of the raw material before export.

Nigeria still has a lot of unrealized potential for cash crop production. Cocoa constitutes a small proportion of Nigerian exports. Cotton is also produced for export, but Nigeria is developing the industry for domestic demand as well. Tobacco, rice, coffee, and kola nuts, which are used in the manufacture of cola drinks, are produced for domestic demand.

Many types of grain and vegetables are grown as subsistence crops. Farmed on a large scale, these crops have the potential to become major sources of income for the country. Cattle farming is largely practiced in the north by the nomadic Fulani, who are encouraged with the aid of irrigation projects to settle down and raise cattle commercially. Other irrigation projects have led to rice farming in the Sokoto area and the cultivation of rice, wheat, and cotton around the previously unused shores of Lake Chad.

Agriculture has suffered from years of mismanagement, inconsistent and poorly conceived government policies, neglect and the lack of basic infrastructure. Still, the sector accounts for over 35.4 percent of GDP. Nigeria is no longer a major exporter of cocoa, groundnuts (peanuts), rubber, and palm oil. Cocoa production, mostly from obsolete varieties and overage trees, is stagnant at around 198,416 short tons (180,000 metric tons) annually;

Nigerian man tending young palm oil trees on a farm.

Agriculture accounts for two-thirds of all employment.

25 years ago it was 330,693 short tons (300,000 tons). An even more dramatic decline in groundnut and palm oil production also has taken place. Once the biggest poultry producer in Africa, corporate poultry output has been slashed from 40 million birds annually to about 18 million. Import constraints limit the availability of many agricultural and food processing inputs for poultry and other sectors. Fisheries are poorly managed. Most critical for the country's future, Nigeria's land tenure system does not encourage long-term investment in technology or modern production methods and does not inspire the availability of rural credit. Agriculture has failed to keep pace with Nigeria's rapid population growth, so that the country, which once exported food, now relies on imports to sustain itself.

Nigeria has three oil refineries, all owned by the Nigerian National Petroleum Company, NNPC.

OIL

Britain was the chief beneficiary of Nigerian oil in the early years of the colony's oil industry. After gaining independence, Nigeria expanded its oil export destinations to include Western European nations, especially Germany, and the United States.

By 1974 Nigeria had become the world's ninth-largest oil producer, and oil provided 80 percent of the country's foreign exchange earnings. Nigeria benefits from the high quality of its oil, the relative stability of its oil production, and its ties with Western markets.

Most of Nigeria's oil companies were originally foreign-owned, with only 50 percent of the profits going to the state. Foreign companies also chose to import skilled labor and equipment rather than develop them locally. Successive governments in Nigeria have passed legislation insisting on a greater share of the profits and on the use of local labor. That became a point of contention between the companies and the government in the 1970s that resulted in oil shortages.

NATURAL GAS

When oil is drilled, natural gas is released as a by-product. For decades Nigeria has been pumping up oil and burning off the accompanying natural gas, when the gas has economic potential and could support a lucrative bottled gas and plastics industry. However, the cost of setting up the infrastructure for such an industry is very high, and plans to do it have been shelved many times. Today, Nigeria's natural gas products industry is taking off, which should open up new export markets and employment opportunities.

Nigeria is heavily dependent on oil, which accounts for 95 percent of the country's exports, totaling $15 billion a year. Nigeria supplies 22 million tons of oil a year to the European Union and 8 percent of all U.S. oil imports. It is possible that Nigeria has larger oil reserves even than Iraq, but the Nigerian oil industry suffers serious political problems.

Poor corporate relations with indigenous communities, vandalism of oil infrastructure, severe ecological damage, and personal security problems throughout the Niger Delta oil-producing region continue to plague Nigeria's oil sector. Efforts are underway to reverse these troubles. In the absence of government programs, the major multinational oil companies have launched their own community development programs. A new entity, the Niger Delta Development Commission (NDDC), has been created to help catalyze economic and social development in the region. Although it has yet to launch its programs, hopes are high that the NDDC can reverse the impoverishment of local communities.

Nigeria's proven oil reserves are estimated to be 36 billion barrels; natural gas reserves are well over 100 trillion cubic feet.

TRADITIONAL HANDICRAFTS

Traditional Nigerian handicrafts form the basis of a small but flourishing industry. In Benin, home to some magnificent ancient bronzes, there are guilds that control the production of iron implements and ivory, ebony, and wood carvings.

Oyo is the center for carved calabashes—large hollowed-out gourds that are made into water vessels. Some of the vessels are strong enough to hold boiling water.

TEXTILES Most of the Nigerian cotton crop is produced for local consumption. Cotton fabrics are produced mostly in Kaduna state. The climate of the north supports the cultivation of cotton on small farms. It is a very labor-intensive industry, requiring the handpicking of cotton bolls. Inside the boll, the seeds are covered in a mass of white fibers that twist as they dry, allowing thread to be spun. The cotton is made into brightly patterned cloth.

Women and young girls harvesting cotton by hand into bundles in a field.

THE FUTURE

Until it can produce locally items that it still imports, Nigeria will remain dependent on other countries and have a large import bill. Processing plants exist for materials that were traditionally exported to Europe, but the manufacturing industry is weak.

Nigeria's industrial centers are Lagos, Port Harcourt, Enugu, Benin, Kano, and Kaduna. There are assembly plants for several models of cars, but the parts are not manufactured in Nigeria.

If Nigeria is to process, it has to eradicate corruption and base its economy on competition and private enterprise. Successive military governments have systematically looted the nation's wealth, giving valuable contracts for economic development projects to members of the military or to their supporters with no regard to the cost.

Nigeria also has to create a safe environment for foreign investors. Reports of riots in Nigeria fill the foreign press. Agricultural production is at an all-time low although the country has the capacity to feed itself and export to other African nations.

While the cost of building infrastructure to enable economic growth is high, Nigeria does have the natural resources it needs. How problems of the present are managed will determine the country's economic future.

The production of cotton in Nigeria has declined to 132,277 short tons (120,000 metric tons) per annum, which is less than half of over 330,693 short tons (300,000 metric tons) per annum once produced in Nigeria.

INTERNET LINKS

www.economywatch.com/world_economy/nigeria/

Comprehensive statistics on Nigeria's economy.

www.nigerianeconomicsociety.org/

The official website of the Nigerian economic society with links to articles and papers on Nigeria's economy.

www.infoplease.com/ce6/world/A0860003.html

A concise overview of Nigeria's economy.

ENVIRONMENT

A rural school in the remote mountainous region of Nigeria.

5

RAPID ECONOMIC DEVELOPMENT and a fragile political situation have caused serious environmental problems in Nigeria. Waste generated by a growing population and industries such as oil and mining pollutes air, land, and water.

Expanding farmland and the demand for timber causes deforestation and land deterioration. Irrigation diverts watercourses and disturbs the ecology of the land.

Ecotourism is important throughout western Africa, and Nigeria has a vested interest in protecting its wildlife. The country's wildlife parks are popular destinations for both foreign and local visitors and have a lot of

Tourists enjoying Wikki Warm Springs at Yankari National Park.

growth potential. National parks, especially the more established ones, such as Yankari and Kainji Lake, are thus important havens for Nigerian wildlife, ensuring plants' and animals' protection at least for their economic appeal.

Nigeria is party to several international agreements on a variety of environmental subjects and fields, such as biodiversity, climate change, desertification, hazardous waste, marine conservation, the nuclear test ban, and the ozone layer.

ENVIRONMENT VERSUS ECONOMY

While ecotourism appears to pull together Nigeria's environmental and economic needs, the country's most significant industry—oil—has done irreversible damage to the natural environment. Oil spills and fires have for years been wreaking havoc on homes, farmland, and nature in and around the Niger Delta. Other industries strain the infrastructure of the urban areas, leading to pollution and waste disposal problems.

Political and social problems hinder Nigeria's efforts to improve infrastructure for waste treatment, proper sanitation, and potable water supplies, and to control the ravages of the oil industry.

DEFORESTATION

Logging has reduced forest cover in Nigeria to an area of about 14,672 square miles (38,000 square km), which is less than 5 percent of the forested area in the early 20th century. It has been predicted that if logging does not slow down, Nigeria will lose all its forest by 2020.

Forests are logged for several reasons, such as for agriculture or to harvest commercially valuable hardwoods. Most Nigerians who live in

One environmental problem Nigeria faces is the air pollution that is caused by burning gas during oil production in the Niger delta.

forested areas are very poor. They cannot afford fossil fuels, so they cut down trees to obtain firewood, their major source of fuel. Peasant farmers practice slash-and-burn cultivation—they clear a site, farm it until it loses fertility, and move to a new site to repeat the process. Companies log large areas of forest using big machines and sell the harvested hardwoods to be made into furniture.

Deforestation has serious consequences. Trees are the life support of forest ecosystems. They protect the soil from erosion, purify the air, provide shelter and food for people and animals, and produce water vapor that forms clouds that fall as rain. Certain species have medicinal value. Deforestation has long-term effects on the future of Nigerians as it changes the landscape, climate, and biodiversity.

Much of the allowance for deforestation in Nigeria comes from their demand for fuel wood.

Nigeria has been losing 988,422 acres (400,000 hectares) of its forest cover every year, or 3.5 percent of its total forested area.

SOIL EROSION

Without shelter from foliage, the ground is exposed to the force of Nigeria's heavy rains. In southern areas where forest cover has been cleared, whole hillsides have disappeared as more and more soil has been carried away by rain. The Jos Plateau is a spectacular example of soil erosion. Its 4,800 miles (7,725 km) of gullies were formed by the movement of an estimated 1 million tons of soil.

Erosion removes topsoil. The land loses fertility and its capacity to retain water. It can no longer support new plant growth and becomes susceptible to drought. Soil erosion causes problems not only where it takes place. Water that is not absorbed into the soil carries away soil particles. The runoff collects in rivers, causing them to silt up or muddy the water downstream.

DYING WATERCOURSES

Despite the massive volume of water flowing through Nigeria in the great Niger and Benue rivers, 50 million Nigerians do not have access to potable water. While the country is investing heavily to improve the situation, many developments have been plagued with problems, and the shortage of usable water continues to worsen with environmental degradation.

There are several reasons why Nigeria's water sources are dying a slow death. Lake Chad in the far northeast is in danger of drying up because of numerous projects by Nigeria and neighboring countries taking water from the rivers that feed the lake.

The dumping of domestic and industrial waste from Lagos city into the Lagos lagoon, which is the city's water supply, leads to outbreak of diseases. For example, in 2001 pollution in Kano's water supply led to a cholera outbreak that claimed more than 600 lives. The environmental protection agency in Lagos requires that industries treat effluents before disposal, but the city lacks adequate sanitation and sewage treatment facilities.

Nigeria's greatest water problem is in the Niger Delta, where oil fields are found. The delta is one of the world's largest wetlands, covering 7,722 square miles (20,000 square km). Formed over centuries by silt washed down the Niger and Benue rivers, it contains threatened forest, islands, freshwater swamp, and mangrove.

Making up almost 97 percent of Nigeria's export earnings, Nigerian oil comes mostly from fields in and around the Niger Delta. Foreign companies and the Nigerian state company operate in the delta and offshore fields. The oil industry has had a devastating effect on the delta's ecology. Oil spills and fires have polluted the water, damaged farmland and fisheries, and destroyed wildlife.

In 1993 a major spill in the Ogoni Territory of the delta region, spread by summer rains, polluted the Osadegha river and destroyed vast areas of arable land. In 1998 a spill from a burst pipeline flooded the Oyara mangrove with crude oil. In 2001 oil fires in the Ogoni Territory destroyed homes and crops and left the land permanently barren.

One approach that the government has taken to discourage oil spills in the Niger Delta is the imposition of hefty fines, to date exceeding $100 million, on oil companies that are responsible for spills.

RECYCLING IN NIGERIA

Recycling in Nigeria has largely been ad-hoc, with scavengers picking up what they can from waste sites and reselling it. However, in 2011, a boom in recycling across the four major dump sites of Lagos opened the government's eyes to the potential of recycling. Lagos generates over 9,000 tons of waste per day. Due to this volume, scavenging has been booming as the rag pickers ransack the four major dumpsites across the state for used items that could be sold and recycled. The government formalized recycling and set up recycling banks at various parts of the state. The figures are encouraging: according to the *Lagos Daily Independent*, at the moment Lagos recycles 18 percent of its waste, and is hoping to increase that percentage in the years to come.

In 2012, Japan and Nigeria set up a partnership to recycle abandoned cars. The recycling plant would be set up in Abuja, and this would not only help clear the Nigerian environment of scrap vehicles but also create jobs, alleviate poverty, and bring wealth through industrialisation.

After a major oil leak from an underground pipe, the waters of **Bodo Creek** are filled with oil forcing farmers and fishermen to move out past the spills in order to provide for their families.

"The story of oil and gas in Africa is the story of rogue exploitation, despoliation, and bizarre brigandage. It is a story of pollution, displacement, and pillage. It is a montage of burnt rivers, burnt forests, and maimed lives. An oil well is a death sentence if it is located in your backyard."

—Nnimmo Bassey
from *Oilwatch*

THE NIGERIAN CONSERVATION FOUNDATION

Formed in 1980, the Nigerian Conservation Foundation (NCF) is Nigeria's oldest and most established wildlife protection agency. It is a nongovernmental organization.

The NCF plans and conducts nature conservation projects and promotes conservation education in Nigeria. It has helped to establish and support game reserves and national parks in the country. The NCF also runs environmental education and awareness programs for schools and the public and works with international environmental organizations such as the World Wildlife Fund (WWF) and the United Nations Environmental Program (UNEP) to protect Nigeria's endangered species.

The NCF aims ultimately to stop and reverse the damage that people have inflicted or are inflicting on Nigerian nature and to help develop a symbiotic relationship between people and nature. The NCF tries to achieve its goals by promoting biodiversity conservation, sustainable development, and pollution and waste reduction. It works to influence policymakers, lobby for important habitats to be declared protected areas, encourage environmental education, and collaborate with governmental and other environmental organizations to promote careful use of natural resources that takes into account the traditions of local communities.

WILDLIFE CONSERVATION

Many of Nigeria's large mammals, such as hyenas, jackals, and wild pigs and dogs, especially in the north, are migrating to other countries due to bush burning, tree felling, and drought.

There are 290 mammal species in Nigeria. Of these, 25 are endangered, including the vulnerable cheetah, lion, red-fronted gazelle, pygmy hippopotamus, African pygmy squirrel, and spotted-necked otter, and the endangered chimpanzee, giant African water shrew, African elephant, and red-bellied monkey.

There are nine threatened species of birds in Nigeria, including the endangered white-throated mountain babbler and the vulnerable corn crake, marbled teal, Anambra waxbill, and Bannerman's weaver.

Nigeria has established wildlife reserves to protect biodiversity. The Yankari National Park in Bauchi state is home to baboons, elephants, waterbuck, and more than 899 species of birds. The Gashaka Gumti Game Reserve in Adamawa state, the largest park in Nigeria, protects several species of primates, hippopotamuses, and birds. Close to Benin city is Okomo, home to a small forest with white-throated monkeys, elephants, and many species of birds.

The Cross River National Park is home to the Cross River gorilla, a subspecies numbering only 150 to 200. The gorilla has been classified as critically endangered by the IUCN. Inside the park, rangers protect the gorillas, but there are also gorillas living in the hills on the Nigeria-Cameroon border outside the park, where poachers hunt them for bushmeat. Protecting the gorilla requires collaboration between the two countries. The illegal bushmeat trade also threatens chimpanzees, as people smuggle the animal carcasses to the West.

The Nigeria-Cameroon chimpanzee is the most endangered of all chimpanzee subspecies and is likely to be extinct in the coming decades.

INTERNET LINKS

www.unep.org/nigeria/

The United Nations Environment Program Organization report on Nigeria.

www.nesrea.org/

The website of the National Environment Standards and Regulation Enforcement Agency (NESREA), an official agency looking after the environment in Nigeria.

http://rainforests.mongabay.com/20nigeria.htm

The statistics on this website will incense you about the state of the environment in Nigeria.

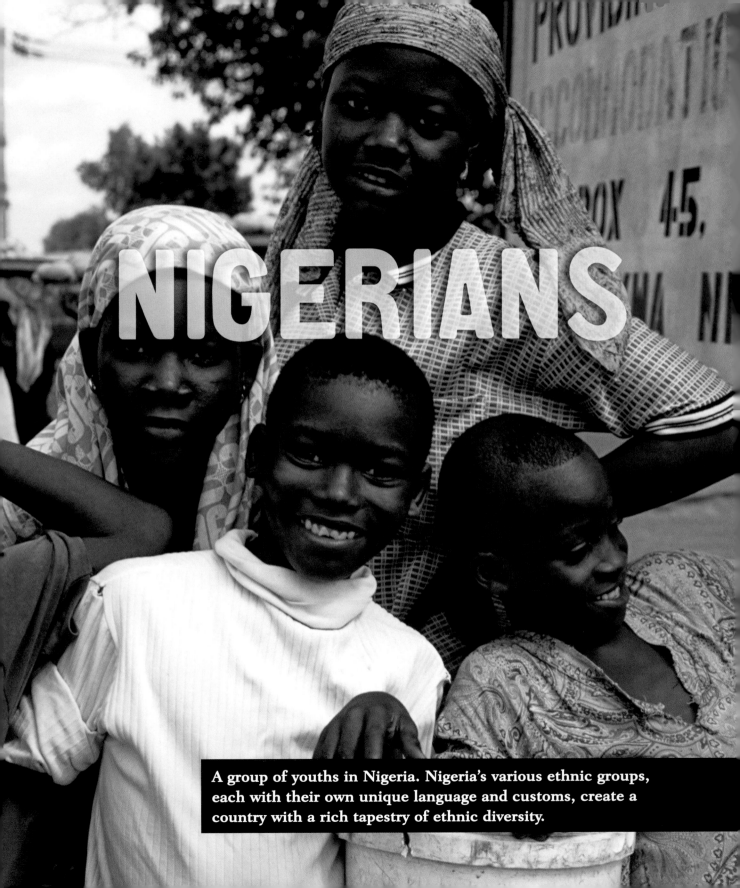

NIGERIANS

A group of youths in Nigeria. Nigeria's various ethnic groups, each with their own unique language and customs, create a country with a rich tapestry of ethnic diversity.

N IGERIANS HAVE LONG struggled with issues of identity. While having created a unique culture, ethnic diversity has also generated tension in the country. The major ethnic groups remain concentrated in large geographical regions. To an extent, state divisions have helped to deemphasize ethnic identities.

Nigerians can be superficially categorized into three major ethnic groups and regions: Hausa-Fulani in the north, Yoruba in the west, and Ibo in the east. The population of Nigeria is in fact made up of many different ethnic groups, each with its own language and religion. Urbanization has further complicated ethnic issues, as the major cities are usually a hodgepodge of ethnic groups.

People in the north, generally Muslim and Hausa-speaking, make up the majority of the Nigerian population. The main occupations in the north are cash crop farming and cattle raising.

There are about 30 million Yoruba in Nigeria. They dominate the southwest and are the majority group in towns such as Lagos and Ibadan. Like the Hausa groups, most Yoruba are farmers living in walled towns who commute to the farms daily.

In the southeast of Nigeria, the dominant group is the Ibo. During colonial times, Ibo people held most of the administrative positions. The Ibo region is probably the least traditional part of Nigeria because of its developed oil industry and the lack of scope for agricultural development there.

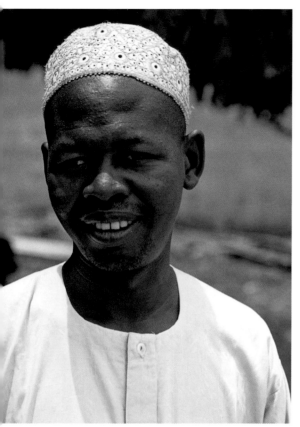

The Hausa are one of the largest ethnic groups in West Africa.

Predominantly Hausa communities are scattered throughout West Africa and on the traditional Hajj (pilgrimage to Mecca) route across the Sahara Desert.

PEOPLE OF THE NORTH

HAUSA There was a complex political system in the Hausa states long before the British arrived in West Africa. Even before the arrival of Islam, competition for trade with states to the north made the Hausa strong, while their lack of a writing system or of shared beliefs kept them from forming an empire.

Around them, the Songhai Empire and the Kanem-Borno kingdom arose, while most Hausa states remained small units. Government in the Hausa states was based on family dynasties until Nigeria's independence.

Present-day Hausa cities form the educational, commercial, social, and administrative centers for the surrounding countryside. Hausa people are primarily farmers, many of whom live in the cities and possess craftmaking skills.

Social status among the Hausa is based on one's degree of urbanization. A person who can afford to live in a town is considered to have a higher status than someone who lives on a farm. The poor become clients of the rich and, in return for loans or other help, offer support in any way they can, often through voting.

FULANI No one knows the origins of the Fulani. They remain largely nomadic, driving their herds of cattle across northern Nigeria in search of grazing and water.

In the 19th century, the Fulani led jihads against corrupt Hausa governments and became rulers of the Hausa.

KANURI The Kanuri represent about 4 percent of the population of Nigeria. Most of them live in the state of Borno, although some live in towns and cities farther south or in Niger and Chad. Kanuri culture goes back 1,000 years to the Kanem-Borno kingdom.

Like the Hausa, the Kanuri are Muslims and have a similar system of client-patron relations. That would once have had a military purpose but in modern times it means loans or work in exchange for political or financial support.

TIV Neither northerners nor southerners, the Tiv are a curious people, defying the understanding of outsiders. Before Nigerian independence, Tiv political structure was unlike any other in the country. They had no chiefs, no administrative structure, and no identifiable leaders. They existed peacefully with one another because of genealogical ties.

There are few Tiv towns, since they are traditionally a rural people. During 1991 and 1992, the Tiv nearly went to war with the neighboring Jukun people over political boundaries.

PEOPLE OF THE EAST

IBO The Ibo consist of as many as 200 smaller groups. For many years of Ibo history, they fought with and took slaves from one another. The typical Ibo settlement was tiny, with 2,000 people at most.

Colonized by the British later than the people of the western states, the Ibo accepted missionary education and spread throughout Nigeria in the administrative ranks and in the handicraft industry. Most Ibo became Christians and were favored by the colonial power.

However, the Ibo came to be deeply resented by other local groups, particularly in the north, who felt under-privileged. In the 1960s, huge massacres of Ibo people took place in the north, and the Ibo began to migrate back to Iboland in the east, where for the first time a sense of Ibo unity was born.

Covering lands rich in oil, and with the biggest oil refinery in Nigeria, Iboland could easily have stood independently from the rest of the country. Indeed, in 1967 the Ibo seceded from Nigeria, setting up the independent Republic of Biafra.

But things did not go well. The Nigerian government enjoyed the support of the international community, while the Republic of Biafra received no

Kanuri groups have traditionally been sedentary, engaging in farming, fishing the Lake Chad basin, and engaging in trade and salt processing.

Traditional dress varies across ethnic groups. If the traditional dress of the north is Arab-influenced, that of the southeast is African-influenced.

Women in the southeast typically wear a loose blouse on top, a piece of cloth wrapped around the lower body and folded at the waist, and a piece of cloth folded around the head. Men in the southeast wrap a large piece of cloth around the lower body and twist it into many folds at the waist.

In the north, men usually wear a floor-length robe, heavily embroidered in the front, over baggy cotton or silk drawstring pants. They also wear a skullcap, or fez. Wearing loose clothes helps keeps them cool, and pants make it easy to ride a horse, traditionally used for transportation and warfare in the north. Women in the north wear dark-colored clothing that covers the whole body, with headgear that can also be worn as a veil.

Nigerians also wear Western-style clothing such as shirts, trousers, skirts, blouses, dresses, and suits.

support from neighboring countries, where governments faced a similar threat of secession from disaffected peoples.

Rather than surrender, the Ibo slowly starved to death. Finally, after thousands had died, the Ibo admitted defeat. The Nigerian government took no reprisals against them, and today there is officially no prejudice against the Ibo as a result of the Biafran War.

Nevertheless, the suffering of the Ibo remains fresh in their memory, and there is a general feeling among them that they have been left out of the Nigerian government.

IBIBIO The Ibibio are the second-largest ethnic group in eastern Nigeria. There are about a million Ibibio living mostly on the western side of the Cross River. Their homeland lies south and east of Iboland and north of the coastal delta. The main Ibibio towns are Aba and Uyo.

The method of farming used by the Ibibio is called slash-and-burn cultivation. An area of jungle is cleared by cutting and burning the vegetation. It is farmed until it becomes infertile and then left fallow to revert back to jungle until it is ready to be farmed again.

The main cash crop of the Ibibio is palm oil, although subsistence vegetables such as manioc, corn, cocoyams, and squash are also grown. With the decrease in palm oil production, many Ibibio have become migrant laborers, particularly on oil rigs.

Like the Ibo, the Ibibio have only recently come to see themselves as an ethnic unit. In the past, fighting between villages was common.

PEOPLE OF THE WEST

YORUBA The Yoruba live in an area of the Lagos, Ondo, Oyo, Ogun, Osun, Ekiti, and some parts of Kwara and Edo states. The Yoruba make their living from fishing and from growing palm oil, cocoa, yams, cocoyams, bananas, corn, guinea corn, cassava, and plantains.

The Yoruba are predominantly town dwellers. A typical Yoruba town has high walls and a ditch, with a centrally placed royal palace alongside the town market. Each large kinship group lives in a compound with a large, rectangular courtyard. Originally animists, the Yoruba have converted in almost equal numbers to Christianity and Islam.

Traditionally, the Yoruba people were ruled by kings, each township with its own ruler. During the height of the slave trade, Yoruba kings declined in power to be replaced by traders with private armies. But the arrival of the

Due to the effects of migration and the Atlantic slave trade, there are descendant ethnic Ibo populations in countries outside Africa. Their exact population outside Africa is unknown, but today many African Americans and Afro Caribbeans are of Ibo descent.

Yoruba dress reflects the influence of many different cultures. Christian Yoruba men dress more Western-style. Muslim Yoruba men wear Hausa-style clothing and several silk or cotton gowns over that, the final layer being a highly pleated agbada *(ahg-BAHD-ah).*

The agbada *drapes from the shoulders to fall below the knees and is made of the same cloth as the trousers. The wealthier the man, the more layers of clothing he wears and the more ornate the design and finish.*

Yoruba women wear a skirt called an irobirin *(eer-o-BEER-in). It is 15 feet (4.5 m) of cloth wrapped in different patterns around the hips to drape toward one side. The* irobirin *is topped by a simple square-shaped blouse and covered by another piece of cloth draped over the left shoulder. Yoruba women traditionally wear a gele (GAY-lay), which is a head tie that takes many different shapes according to the fashion of the time. It is said that the way a woman wears her gele reveals her attitude and mood.*

British reinstated the kings, as theirs was the administrative system that best suited the colonial power.

Today, the Yoruba practice polygamy. If he can afford it, a Yoruba man will have many wives. All his sons will inherit his wealth equally, so it is difficult for single, wealthy dynasties to emerge.

Modern, well-educated Yoruba no longer live in the communities in which they were born. About a fifth of them live in the bigger cities, particularly Lagos and Ibadan. They work in government administration or in companies, where they earn wages rather than work as farmers. Nevertheless, they maintain links with their homeland.

EDO The Edo occupy the land from the city of Benin to the Niger River. Like the Yoruba, the Edo are largely farmers, using the slash-and-burn technique of farming to make a living out of the fragile tropical soil. A new garden is cleared out of the rain forest every season, and the previous one is left to revert to its original state.

In Edo society, even farming jobs are sharply differentiated. The men are responsible for cutting and burning the natural vegetation and for tending the yam crop, while the women look after the other crops.

Edo is also the name of the language that the Edo speak. Smaller groups of Edo live around Benin and are called the Bini. They are the descendants of the sophisticated civilization of Benin that was ruled for hundreds of years by the Oba, the sacred ruler. More than 3.8 million Nigerians live in the Edo state. Many trace their roots to ancient Benin, and there are similarities in cuisine, clothing, and customs.

A 17th century account of Benin by a Flemish writer describes it as 5 miles (8 km) in circumference, with a beautiful palace in the center and 30 large streets crossed by many smaller ones. When the British sacked Benin in 1897 in reprisal for the massacre of trade missionaries, they discovered exquisite bronzes, carved ivory tusks, and masks of great beauty and value.

INTERNET LINKS

www.nairaland.com/158215/pictures-nigeria-traditional-attire

A lovely page with gorgeous pictures of traditional Nigerian attire.

http://yeyeolade.wordpress.com/2009/05/15/geles-yoruba-head-dress-headties-from-yoruba-nigeriaand-blackamerikkka/

A page on the *gele* (head tie) which shows an amazing number of ways to tie the *gele* on one's head.

www.news.bbc.co.uk/2/hi/africa/596712.stm

A historical look at the Biafran war from the British Broadcasting Corporation news.

LIFESTYLE

The calabash (hard shell gourd) fruit is widely used in Nigeria as a kitchen utensil and container for storing medicine and food.

A DETAILED DESCRIPTION of lifestyles in modern Nigeria would fill volumes. Like other developing countries undergoing massive change, Nigeria has been catapulted into the 21st century.

While ethnic ties have an influence on life in Nigeria, on a day-to-day basis urban Nigerians live in a manner typical of people in industrialized societies. They go shopping in supermarkets, use modern appliances at home, eat Western foods, and relax at the movies or a nightclub. They commute to work and complain about the traffic.

In contrast, Nigerians who live in rural areas follow a very traditional way of life and have different expectations and values from those of Nigerians who live in urban areas. For example, the Fulani move from place to place with the rains, and their prosperity depends on the health of their cattle herds. In the far north, women in Borno state might stay home all day and see no one but their husbands.

BIRTH AND CHILDHOOD

Among the Muslim groups, such as the Hausa, Kanuri, and Fulani, birth ceremonies are observed according to Islamic law with some ethnic additions. When giving birth, a Hausa woman stays in her husband's compound and is ritually compelled by his kinswomen to nurse the newborn. Following the birth of her first child, the mother goes to her parents' compound for a few days. Ritual washing is done for several months after giving birth. On the seventh day of life, the child is named in an Islamic ceremony, and a ram is sacrificed. The child is breastfed for two years and then put in the care of an older sister. All children live in

7

The average Nigerian can expect to live 52.1 years. By contrast, the average American citizen can expect to live 78.5 years.

In the past, the death rate among Nigerian babies was very high, and this factor influenced the rituals surrounding the birth of a child. As in many other African communities, a big family is desired by everyone, so that the parents will be well cared for in their old age. In 2012 the infant mortality rate in Nigeria was 74 for every 1,000 births.

the women's section of the compound, but boys who are old enough to help in the fields move to the men's living area.

The Fulani consider a child to be a year old at birth and to have no identity until given a name. Until the child is named, he or she is called it. The child's name is determined by the day of birth. In polygamous families, children have little contact with their father, although the sons expect to inherit from him. Kinship is with the family of the mother rather than that of the father.

Among the Ibo, it is traditionally believed that a newborn is inhabited by the spirit of someone who has died. The spirit may decide to stay in the new body or leave. It is not until the child starts walking and talking that the spirit is assumed to have decided to stay. The Ibo once believed that the birth of twins was an abomination, and a mother and her twin children would be driven out of the village.

PUBERTY AND ADOLESCENCE

As children grow older, there are several significant moments for them connected with family life. Nigerian children tend to be initiated into adulthood at a younger age than their Western counterparts.

In Hausa society, boys undergo circumcision, which begins their preparation for adulthood, at about age 7. Marriage marks the start of adulthood, although going to work might be more of a distinction in Western terms.

The Hausa bride and groom traditionally do not have to be present at the marriage ceremony. Hausa marriage rituals last several days. The bride-to-

FEMALE GENITAL MUTILATION

The Ibo have a practice of scarring and circumcising young girls who are entering adolescence. This practice, known as Female Genital Mutilation, is condemned as brutal and a deadly health risk by the World Health Organization (WHO). Happily, on February 6, 2012, International Day of Zero Tolerance to Female Genital Mutilation/Cutting (FGM/C), showed that social norms and cultural practices are changing, and communities are uniting to protect the rights of girls and women against the harmful tradition.

be has her skin stained with henna and goes into seclusion for some time to receive the necessary instructions before marriage.

As part of the marriage rituals, the bride-to-be shows her modesty and reluctance to become a bride by trying to escape from her seclusion. No such rituals are performed if the bride or groom divorce and remarry.

In Fulani tradition, a boy comes of age when he is circumcised. He moves from the women's quarters to an area designated for unmarried men and is given his own cattle, a staff, and some Koranic charms.

Fulani women, such as these pictured above, will eventually go on to marry and start their own families.

There are several other rituals that Fulani youth experience. For example, it is customary for Fulani boys approaching marriageable age to ritually beat one another in order to prove their strength and thus suitability as husbands.

At puberty, Fulani boys and girls learn to flirt and perform special dances in the marketplace. The eligible boys dance and sing a praise song in which they describe the charms of the eligible girls. That indicates how each girl ranks among the boys in terms of desirability for marriage. The girls also perform a dance, and when they find a boy that they like, they stop dancing and stand by him.

THE MARKETPLACE

In Nigeria, the marketplace is the focal point of the village or town and often the sole reason for its existence. Even today, after the massive changes brought about by Nigeria's newfound wealth, many people produce, transport, and sell their own goods. A Yoruba woman might make pots or cloth, or she might have a surplus of vegetables that she wishes to sell. The final price she gets for her products determines how well she and her children

Most Nigerians still prefer to shop at the traditional markets.

will eat or how good their education will be. Consequently she drives a hard bargain at the marketplace.

In the bigger cities, whole markets exist only for the sale of one type of item. In Ibadan there is a cloth market, a soap market, a food market, and a handicraft market. These are in addition to the other many daily markets whose function changes as the day progresses. In the morning, the original producer or a middleman sells produce to the regular stallholders. In the afternoon, the stallholders sell to the housewives. At night, the food hawkers open their stalls to cater to the local nightlife.

Traditionally, Ibo society did not have the structure that the West associates with government. Leadership went to those who had proved their skills in other areas and could not be inherited or canvassed for. In 1929 the colonial government taxed Ibo men on their property for the first time. It was a shock to discover that they had to give money to a government—something they had no concept of and had never previously needed.

When in the following year the same authorities began a survey of the property of women, a spontaneous resistance movement began. Unarmed women marched through villages. In Calabar and Opobo, some court buildings were attacked. The government ordered troops to open fire, and on December 16, 1929, many women were killed—53 in Calabar province alone.

The riots were unsuccessful, but they led to a reorganization of tax laws.

THE ROLE OF WOMEN

In the countryside, many old ways still survive. Ibo women traditionally leave their villages to marry, and consequently women rarely own land. Inheritance is through the male line. In traditional Ibo culture, women process palm oil and trade in the local markets. That gives them an opportunity to sell surplus crops and exchange news with women from their home village.

In traditional Hausa society, men do most of the agricultural and handicraft work, leaving women with the domestic work—weaving cotton, making blankets, and making sweets. The markets are also dominated by men, unlike in Yoruba and Ibo societies.

Single women have the option of becoming praise singers, or *jakadiya* (ja-ka-DEE-ya) messengers. Hausa women are the chief devotees and exponents of the cult of spirit possession.

Polygamy is the normal practice in traditional Hausa society. It dates back to the time of tribal warfare, when many men died and polygamy offered protection to widows. Islamic law allows a man to have several wives, with the first having the greatest status. However, monogamy is becoming common with education and the influence of Christianity.

WOMEN'S RIGHTS

By Western standards, women in Nigeria lack protection. Particularly in the northern states, women suffer serious human rights violations.

Since 1999, states such as Katsina and Sokoto have been ruled by an extremist interpretation of Islamic law that allows for women to be sentenced to death by stoning on charges of adultery. In 2002 a young mother, Amina Lawal, was so sentenced for having her child out of wedlock. Her case was closely monitored by Amnesty International. Her acquittal in 2003 was a victory for women's rights in Nigeria.

Upper-class woman wearing traditional headgears in Port Harcourt.

Women in Nigeria's cities fare better. Many are employed in light industry and see self-improvement as a goal. Also, more marriages are monogamous. Women's Rights Watch Nigeria aims to help Nigerian women whose human rights have been violated through, for example, circumcision, domestic violence, or unjust laws.

MARRIAGE

There are three forms of marriage in Nigerian society: the traditional marriage in the woman's home; the official marriage in a registry office; and the religious marriage. The official marriage allows a man only one wife, and the rites of the religious marriage depend on the couple's religion. Christian marriages in Nigeria are similar to those in the West, while Islamic marriages allow a man up to four wives.

In Yoruba marriages, the man chooses a wife from his community. If his parents approve, they help him assemble the bride price. His family visits the bride's house with gifts, and the betrothal is made. The groom then owes duty to his future parents-in-law in terms of help in the fields. Part of the bride price is traditionally spent on equipment for the new home, while the rest is shared by the girl's family.

The wedding is a colorful affair with traditional music and dance. A hotel reception might mark the wedding of wealthy urbanites. In traditional marriages, wife and husband live separately and remain financially independent of each other. In a polygamous marriage, the wives take turns to prepare their husband's meals. They serve him by doing their household chores.

Marriages are arranged along slightly different lines among the Fulani. The boy and girl, both of a similar age, are often betrothed at puberty. The boy's father's representative and a witness visit the camp of the prospective bride and negotiate terms.

A traditional wedding ceremony in Nigeria.

This is followed by a feast at the girl's camp, where a bull is slaughtered and eaten. As soon as the girl is old enough, the betrothal ceremony takes place at the girl's family's camp. They provide the food. When the bride moves to her husband's camp, she is showered in milk, struck with the branches of the Fulani blessing tree, and "threatened" with a grain pestle.

The girl spends her days with her mother-in-law, while the boy continues to tend the family's herd of animals.

As soon as the girl is pregnant, she returns to her father's camp, where she stays to observe the rites of pregnancy and childbirth. She does not return to her husband for two and a half years. They are then considered parents and herders with their own herds and homestead.

When a man dies, it is not uncommon for his wife to go to his next brother, bringing some of his property and other belongings, and marry the brother. Usually, however, the woman will return to her own family upon her husband's death.

THE WEDDING DRESS In the traditional eastern Nigerian wedding, after the bride-to-be has concluded her fattening period, she gets an elaborate hairdo for the wedding day. Her hair is wound into discs around her head and built up into high crests supported by a structure of sticks. A mixture of clay, charcoal, and palm oil is used to stiffen the hair so that it stays together. The bride-to-be takes a piece of cloth covered in bells and cowrie shells and wraps it around her hips, tying it at the waist.

The Ibo, influenced by the British, have a more conservative style for the bride. She wears the wedding cloth suspended from under the arms. Her legs are covered in brass spirals, which are made and fitted by a blacksmith specifically for the ceremony, to be removed later. Other anklets fitted for the wedding will stay on after the ceremony. The ceremony also involves the presentation of a larger piece of cloth, which will be worn around the bride's hips.

In precolonial Nigeria, the wedding was preceded in many groups by a period of preparation and instruction for the future bride. During that time, the bride stayed in a fattening room where she was fed very well so that she would gain a lot of weight by the time of the wedding. Her fatness was considered to indicate health. However, in modern Nigeria fattening is unfashionable. In the fattening room, the bride's only occupation, besides eating, was to learn the *iria* (IR-ee-ah) dance styles. Her departure from the room was marked by a ceremony in which she wore a special dress and hairstyle.

Fattening rooms are also a tradition in the Niger Delta area. The bride-to-be is secluded for 18 months from puberty. She wears a blouse, and a hat made from coral beads and gold, and wraps a short piece of cloth, usually made from expensive Indian imported silk, around her hips. She also wears coral beads, bells, and other ornaments around her neck and ankles and diagonally across her chest. Among some groups, the bride carries a red parrot feather in her mouth to keep her from talking.

Muslim or Christian Nigerians dress according to the marriage customs of their religion.

DIVORCE Divorce is common in Nigeria. Particularly in rural areas, women are completely economically dependent on their husbands. If they seek a divorce to marry another man, the second husband will repay the bride price to the first husband.

Some women may go through several marriages during their lives. There is little conflict between divorcing parties and no social stigma attached to either them or their children. The traditional Nigerian notion of marriage is that of an economic and genealogical rather than an emotional and social partnership.

CITY LIFE

Lifestyles in Nigeria's cities are similar to urban lifestyles in the West, especially with the influx of foreign experts bringing new ideas and consumer goods. Lagos city has large department stores, supermarkets, movie theaters, and all the other paraphernalia of city life.

Rapid urbanization has given Nigerian cities a chaotic character. As many Nigerians have left the countryside in search of a better life in the city, urban facilities have been stretched to their limit, and occasional power cuts are accepted as part of life. Small industries have sprung up to provide jobs for the people who travel to and from work in vehicles imported with the country's oil revenues. Heavy traffic congestion often clogs up the maze of streets, and air pollution has become a problem.

A traditional village house is under construction in Kano.

COUNTRY LIFE

In western Nigeria, a typical settlement is a small village with its own market. In the past, people tended to stay in large settlements for protection. More recently, it has become safer and easier to move away from the towns into smaller settlements.

A typical Yoruba village home is made from mud or clay and is rectangular in shape, with a courtyard surrounded by mud walls. The family grows subsistence crops immediately around the house and cash crops farther away. They harvest the cash crops and sell them in the markets. The family cooks outside the home over an open fire or in a wood-fired clay oven.

Ibo settlements are traditionally very small and consist of windowless homes made from bamboo poles. Vines bind the rectangular frame of the home together, and clay seals up the gaps. The roof is made from banana leaves. Ibo settlements are thus well-camouflaged among the surrounding bush.

Country life in Nigeria is based on small-scale farms, with very little use of complex farm machinery or chemical fertilizers.

Lifestyle **73**

FAMILY LIFE

Traditional Nigerian families, especially in the rural areas, believe in having many children to ensure the next generation of the kinship group. In a typical day in the life of a Yoruba family, the women wake up early to prepare food for their children. They take turns preparing their husband's food.

After eating, the man proceeds to work on the crops. His wives have their own work, tending and harvesting crops or processing palm oil harvested from trees in their plot.

After school, the children help with the family's work. The older boys join the father, while the girls and the younger boys join their mothers.

Nigeria's urban families organize their day in a pattern similar to that in cities elsewhere. The parents go to work in a factory or office, and the children spend their day in school.

The Nigerian government and several nonprofit organizations, such as Human Life International, Family Care Association Nigeria, and the Sexuality Information and Education Council of the United States, support family life in Nigeria through family welfare programs, teenage sexuality education, and the provision of family planning facilities.

ISLAMIC FUNERALS

When a Muslim dies, the imam, or mosque official, prays over the body of the deceased and instructs the family of the deceased in the preparation of the body for burial.

Islamic tradition requires that the body be washed, dressed in white, wrapped in a thick mat, and buried close to home. The head of the corpse is turned to face the holy city of Mecca.

REINCARNATION

Many eastern Nigerians, such as the Ibo, Igede, Iyala, and Idomo, believe that when they die they will be reincarnated as members of their mother's or sister's family. To make sure that the reincarnation is successful, many preparations are made, especially to ensure that afflictions of the current life do not accompany the soul into the next one.

If a person was blind in this life, the sap of the ogbagbachiko leaf is squeezed into the eyes, and cotton patches placed over them. If a woman was infertile, a cut is made in her abdomen to ensure that she does not suffer the same fate in the next life.

When a man dies, his head is turned to face east so that he will know when the sun is rising and it is time to go to work. When a woman dies her head is turned to face west so that she will know when the sun sets and her husband's meal needs cooking.

For burial, black soil is used to cover the corpse, because red soil is believed to bring skin blemishes in the next life.

FUNERALS

It is thought among eastern Nigerians that the more music, dance, and ceremony that accompany a funeral, the better are the chances for the deceased to enter the afterlife. Consequently, it is considered prudent to provide well for one's own funeral.

The amount of effort put into a funeral varies with the social status of the deceased. A woman's funeral is a brief affair, with the masquerades and

Some Nigerians think that during the course of a funeral the person's ancestors are present among those attending.

dances taking place at her father's compound, not in the public meeting ground. Children and adolescents also get less ostentatious funerals. For men, the degree of ceremony depends on wealth, age, and social status.

Among the Ibo, when a man dies, his wife openly displays her grief, while other women try to calm her down. Respected members of the village are given very elaborate funerals. The wife of a man of status is expected to not lament his death until other respected members of the village have confirmed his death. The funeral ceremony may even be delayed until after the burial in order to give the village time to prepare.

Before the ceremony, a chicken is sacrificed over the slit drum that is to be played. The drum represents the voice of the ancestors, and the sacrifice is said to improve its tone. A burial cloth in the meeting ground represents the deceased.

During the ceremony, the eldest son breaks a pot, symbolizing the release of the deceased into the afterlife. The various social clubs of the village perform dances before the climax—masquerades. Feasting and toasts to the deceased follow. Finally, a diviner checks that everything went well for the soul of the deceased, and the funeral is over.

VALUES

There are some uniform values among Nigerians but also some that are unique to particular groups.

THE HAUSA ETHOS The traditional Hausa value system emphasizes thrift, hard work, patience, restraint, fortitude in adversity, pride in workmanship, and good social relations. Another factor that influences Hausa social behavior is the notion of shame, which compels people to conform to the norms of their society.

IBO BELIEFS The Ibo are a strong-willed and aggressive people who flourished under the colonial government. Their traditional forms of government provided checks and balances that prevented individuals from assuming too much power.

According to indigenous Ibo beliefs the spirits of ancestors and the spirit of the earth influence people's behavior, bringing harm to those who misbehave.

THE FULANI WAY The Fulani Way means the fulfillment of a man's duties toward his elders, wives, and siblings. The Fulani economy is fragile, and the needs of the family and of the herd are in a delicate balance. In hard times, cattle may be sacrificed in order to pay for the needs of the family. This depletes the herd and threatens the wealth of future generations. In moral terms, the Fulani Way calls for modesty, patience, and forethought—qualities that ensure the herds are cared for, the gods appeased, and difficulties endured.

TWINS The Yoruba consider twins sacred and always give them the same names: Taiwo and Kehinde. Traditionally, if one twin died, a wooden statue of the twin would be put on the family shrine. Today, it is more common for Yoruba families to make a trick photograph, using two pictures of the living twin put on the shrine. The Yoruba attitude toward twins is in direct contrast to that of the Ibo, who once considered twins an abomination and drove the mother from the village

INTERNET LINKS

www.womenforwomen.org/global-initiatives-helping-women/help-women-nigeria.php

An enlightening page about the women of Nigeria, and the initiatives taken to help them.

www.maobongoku.com/maobong_mypeople_tradition_fattening.htm

An interesting page about the fattening room, complete with pictures of costumes and the bride at the end of it all.

www.igboguide.org/HT-chapter11.htm

Descriptions and pictures of Ibo wedding and funeral ceremonies.

Flouting the Fulani Way is unthinkable, and the wrongdoer can be banished from Fulani society.

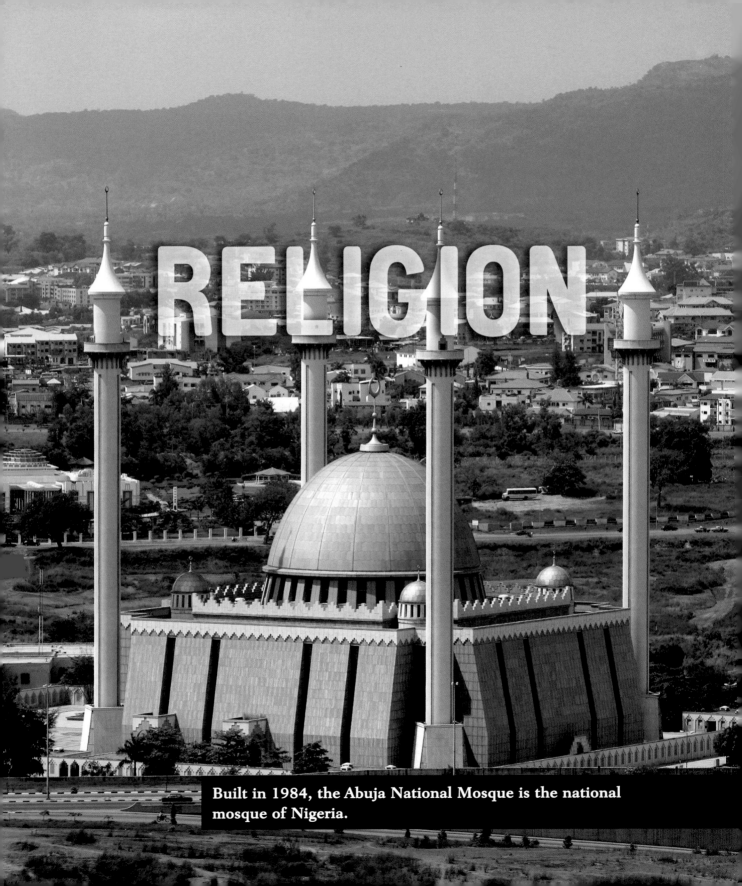

RELIGION

Built in 1984, the Abuja National Mosque is the national mosque of Nigeria.

AS MUCH AS RELIGION is a system of beliefs, it has also been used to further political causes in Nigeria as in many other nations.

Before the arrival of Islam and Christianity, groups in Nigeria followed indigenous animistic religions. They believed in a god whom they could approach in several ways and who was represented on earth by powerful spirits that took the form of objects in the natural environment.

The locals made religious sacrifices or gestures to rivers, mountains, or trees, which they believed were manifestations of the spirits. They attributed the good or harm a river, such as the Niger, did during floods or dry spells to a force beyond the physical.

Osun-Osogbo is a sacred forest viewed as being the residence of the fertility goddess, Osun. The forest itself is full of shrines, works of art, sanctuaries, and sculptures.

8

Very broadly, half of the population of Nigeria is Muslim, 40 percent of the population is Christian, and 10 percent of the people have indigenous beliefs.

Muslim girls study the Koran at an Islamic school in Kano.

Islam first came to Nigeria during the Middle Ages, when it was introduced by the trans-Sahara trading caravans. The religion was widely embraced in the north of the country by rulers quick to perceive the power that its administrative systems would bring. Various Muslim kings dominated the Hausa and Kano states, but a series of Fulani-led jihads reestablished a purer form of Islamic law as empires became corrupt or lost sight of the Islamic way.

Christianity was a later import. Missionaries came with the colonial rulers and set up schools. One condition of admission was conversion to Christianity. As the European traders gradually extended their influence from the southern coast, so the missionary influence spread inland. The southern half of Nigeria thus became largely Christian. Unlike Muslims, many Christians in Nigeria today have animist leanings, since Christianity has not had as much time to replace indigenous practices.

TIV RELIGION

The Tiv have held out the longest against the influx of foreign religions in Nigeria. In its original form, the Tiv religion held that a human being had three elements: body, soul (manifested in a person's shadow), and personality. The Tiv believe that the soul, or *jijingi* (ji-JING-ee), is important because it will go to heaven and it will be inherited by the deceased's children.

In the Tiv system of belief, when God created the world he also created *akombo* (a-KOM-boh), forces in nature that could help or harm people. Within the strongest and most creative individuals in each village, God placed something called *tsav* (sahv), the power to manipulate these forces either for good or evil.

Consequently, it is believed, people can become bewitched by a person with *tsav*. Community elders endowed with *tsav* would fight witches to counteract their deeds. In the past, that involved ritual human sacrifice and cannibalism.

TRADITIONAL BELIEFS

Nigeria's indigenous religions have in common the idea of a single god who, having created the earth and laid down its laws, gave people freedom to choose their paths in life.

No one in Nigeria in the late 20th century can ignore modern scientific knowledge or the pressures of the greater religions, but old beliefs continue to have an influence. Anthropologists are probably better able than the indigenous groups themselves to present a good idea of some of the old ways. But elements of the old religions still exist and have even come to influence the modern religions.

YORUBA RELIGION

The traditional Yoruba system of beliefs includes hundreds of deities associated with mythical figures or landscape features. The Yoruba call their creator Olòrún. They try to appease their ancestors, who they believe can influence their lives from beyond the grave.

By the 1950s, only about 13 percent of Yoruba professed to being followers of indigenous cults. Most were either Muslim or Christian.

IBO RELIGION

The Ibo assumed the religion of the Christian missionaries during the British colonial era in Nigeria. Since the Ibo no longer practice their original religion, our knowledge of their indigenous beliefs and practices is based almost solely on anthropological accounts.

The traditional Ibo religion was polytheistic, that is, it did not include the notion of a supreme being. The early Ibo worshiped many different gods and spirits, including *erosi* (er-OH-see), spirits inhabiting aspects of nature, and *ale* (AH-lay), the spirit of the earth.

The Ibo believed that their ancestors were reincarnated as their descendants, and that in spirit form their ancestors could influence the living. Hence, the Ibo tried to appease their ancestors' spirits so that they could seek help from them in times of need.

The Yoruba religion believes that all human beings possess what is known as *Àyànmô* (destiny, fate) and are expected to eventually become one in spirit with Olòrún, the divine creator and source of all energy.

According to Ibo beliefs, some ancestors become evil spirits and never return to a body but instead haunt their descendants. No one can tell how a spirit is going to turn out. A perfectly good, kind person could turn into an evil spirit.

It is believed that a bad spirit, or jinn, can be appeased by sacrifice in a special place where diseased and stillborn babies are left. If that does not work, the persecuted descendant can find out exactly who the ancestor is by consulting a diviner. They will then dig up the ancestor's bones and burn them, thus destroying the bad spirit.

ISLAM

Roughly half of Nigeria's population is Muslim, and most of them live in the north. Islamic practice, as it has been absorbed into indigenous cultures, varies slightly from one group to another, but the essential principles of Islamic belief are observed.

Men praying at the prayer ground of the mud brick mosque in Kano.

> ### THE MALLAMI

The mallami *(ma-LAH-mee) are Muslim men who hold a semiofficial intermediate rank between the imam and the ordinary Muslim. The thousands of* mallami *are not full-time mosque officials. They guide smaller communities, teaching what they know about the Koran and officiating at less important ceremonies.*

The mallami *often offer help in the form of Koranic charms to people who believe that they have been possessed by bad spirits.*

Islam literally means surrender to the will of Allah. Its tenets are found in the Koran, which Muslims believe was dictated by God to the Prophet Muhammad. There is another body of writing called the Sunna, which consists of accounts of Muhammad's actions by his companions.

The basic tenets of Islam were extended by the Koran into 114 units, which provide Muslims with a body of religious law that covers every aspect of life, from intimate personal behavior and dietary prohibitions to crime. Dress is prescribed, and in the case of women the religious law dictates that they should cover all of their body.

Islamic fundamentalism, which has affected people around the world in different periods, made its impact on Nigeria during the 19th century jihads and also after the adoption of an extremist interpretation of Islamic law by the northern states at the end of the 20th century. The adoption of religious law, strongly connected with ideas of regional autonomy, has had a destabilizing effect on the country, with local Christians finding it an imposition on their lives.

Like Muslims everywhere, Nigerian Muslims go to the mosque on Friday at noon. Prayers are led by the imam, and worshipers give alms, usually in the form of donations to the mosque or food for the poor during festivals.

During Ramadan, Muslims fast from dawn to dusk. For many Muslims, the pilgrimage to Mecca is difficult to make because of the cost of the airfare as well as the physical discomfort. For those who can afford to go, the pilgrimage gives them considerable status in society.

CHRISTIANITY

Christianity came to Nigeria as early as the 17th century with Catholic Portuguese traders who first landed on the southern coast. It was an unsuccessful beginning for the faith in Nigeria. The Anglicans, who came with the British traders, were more successful. They set up Anglican schools and clinics in Yoruba and Ibo territory.

Christians who arrived later were the Southern Baptists from America, the Presbyterians, and the Methodists. Generally, the more established the denomination was in England, the less it traveled in Nigeria. Thus, the influence of groups such as the Jehovah's Witnesses and the Seventh-Day Adventists becomes more obvious the farther into the interior of Nigeria one travels.

Although the missionary churches brought education and medical assistance to the people of Nigeria, they were used by the colonialists and thus became identified with them.

Many Nigerians who were devout Christians felt that the church was dominated by their rulers. So African churches began to come into existence.

Christians having a service at a church.

The Christian
Ecumenical Center
in Abuja.

Their quarrel was not with the nature of the religion or with its practices but with a system in which most of the officials of the church were European.

African churches first came into existence in the early 19th century, increasing in number in the 20th century. For the first time, churches were run by Nigerian clergymen supported by Nigerian parishioners. Anglican religious practices were strictly observed, although concessions were made to the values of polygamy and to the rhythms of Nigerian music.

The differences among many of the denominations have to do more with the manner of worship than with any significant differences in faith. For example, the Anglican churches practice the Anglican Communion, a symbolic act remembering the Last Supper, while services in some Protestant denominations are simpler and involve no such ritual.

By the 1960s, the nationalism that had led to the creation of the African churches had also ensured that the original missionary churches were run by Nigerian people.

While looking at local Nigerian religions, it is possible to see a very practical concern for the problems of everyday life. Spirits or ancestors are regularly

Certain Hausa religious practices have been incorporated into Islamic beliefs, because they are perceived to offer unique spiritual benefits. However, fundamentalist Islam does not take kindly to practices such as the Bori spirit-possession cult. Bori spirit-possession practices offer a place for the religiously marginalized.

During a ceremony, members of the cult are said to be possessed by spirits and cured from their illnesses. Participants in the ceremony often enter into a trance and dance, prophesy, and perform remarkable feats. They carry calabashes on their heads to signify that the spirit has entered them. Many dances at Hausa Islamic festivals can be directly related to traditional beliefs in an earth deity.

called upon for help in dealing with problems, such as poor crops or ill health. The Aladura Church is a result of mixing the beliefs of Christianity with some of the beliefs of Nigeria's traditional religions.

In general, Christian Nigerians choose their church according to their social class. The Anglican Church tends to attract those among the educated elite, who hold the values of the West and who see Sunday attendance at church as an expression of their civilization. The new churches tend to be a little less substantial looking and attract poorer people—those who have more need of material help. However, many middle-class Nigerians go to both categories of churches, preferring the excitement and spontaneity of the new churches and the social standing of the older ones. With 20 million members, the Church of Nigeria is the Anglican Communion's second largest province after the Church of England itself. The president of Nigeria, Goodluck Jonathan, is a member of the congregation.

NEW FORMS OF OLD RELIGIONS

Most Nigerians have converted to Islam or Christianity, although neither religion fits neatly into the spirit of the indigenous religions. Most important in the local religions is the kinship group, whether it be the family, extended family, clan, village, or ethnic group. Individual groups appeal to local deities in their own fashion for protection from and help with life's hardships.

All Aladura churches offer an emotional involvement in their services. They have brought into their rituals behavior inherent in local religions, things not traditionally connected with Christian churches.

Divination and oracles play a large part in discovering exactly which spirit or ancestor has been offended and how to deal with it. The newer religions tend to concentrate on the idea of good behavior and of facing life's problems.

In southern Nigeria, the highly ritualized and ceremonial services of the Anglican Church neglect a basic spiritual need of the Nigerian people—dance and music. The Aladura churches, with roots in prayer groups in the established churches in the 1920s, provide for this need. Aladura priests offer their congregations prophecies, protection from witchcraft (often thought to be the cause of illness), and healing. The apostolic group of Aladura churches tends to be a little more reserved, offering pastoral help rather than prophecy, and their services are quieter. One, the Christ Apostolic Church, does not allow polygamy or the use of Western medicine.

The spiritual group of churches offers much more lively services, involving singing, dancing, and street processions. Worshipers wear colorful clothes, and prophets explain dreams. Spirit possession and speaking in tongues are other common features. The spiritual churches allow both polygamy and Western medicine.

Holy communion performed at a Sunday mass of a Roman Catholic church in Kuru.

INTERNET LINKS

www.godpaths.com/yoruba-religion.html

An excellent description of the Yoruba religion together with depictions of the various deities in the religion.

www.igboguide.org/HT-chapter6.htm

A comprehensive guide to the Ibo religion with an audio vocabulary guide and pictures.

www.anglican-nig.org/

The official website of the Anglican church of Nigeria.

LANGUAGE

Even though most ethnic groups prefer to communicate in their own languages, English, being the official language, is widely used for education, business and official purposes.

THE LANGUAGES OF THE Hausa, Ibo, and Yoruba are not the only important languages in the country. Probably somewhere around 100 languages have been or are spoken in the northern region alone. Of those, some are threatened with extinction, while others such as Hausa are common, spoken by many northerners as a second language.

The southern region is just as complicated linguistically. The Ibo languages are mutually unintelligible: that is, one Ibo group cannot understand another although they have the same ancient ethnic origins. The arrival of the British added to the melting pot of languages. The southern parts of Nigeria came under British rule much earlier than the northern parts, so in the south a pidgin developed based on Yoruba or Ibo grammar but using English words.

SOUTHERN LANGUAGES

IBO There are more than 200 Ibo groups in Nigeria, but the variety of dialects spoken means that communication between Ibo groups is not easy. For a while, Ibo was a common language among the surrounding groups, but the division of their region into four states during the 1970s put an end to the use of a shared Ibo language.

9

The number of languages currently estimated and catalogued in Nigeria is 521. This number includes 510 living languages, two second languages without native speakers, and nine extinct languages.

YORUBA A different Yoruba dialect originated in each of 50 Yoruba kingdoms. In the 1820s the first African Anglican bishop, Samuel Ajayi Crowther from the Yoruba-speaking kingdom of Oyo, said he could not understand the Yoruba that he heard in Lagos. However, in recent times Yoruba dialects have tended to merge.

Like Ibo, Yoruba was a local common language for a time and was spoken by people in rural areas near the Yoruba kingdoms. The use of English in education and administration during the colonial era brought their use of Yoruba to an end.

ENGLISH

English was once the official language in southern Nigeria, while Hausa remained the medium of communication and education in the north. In present-day Nigeria, English is the official medium of instruction in all schools, universities, and colleges. It is the language spoken in the courts and government offices, although Hausa is still officially listed as a second national language.

English teacher discussing questions with students at a secondary school in Jos.

For many Nigerians, studying English is the means of moving up the social and professional ladder. Many families speak their indigenous language at home but switch to English in public. English is used in administrative jobs, which are seen by many Nigerians as secure and influential positions. English also helps Nigerians in higher education either at home or abroad.

For many years, Britain was Nigeria's chief trading partner, so English served their business exchanges well. In addition, countries setting up businesses in Nigeria would send employees who spoke English.

Sociologists suggest that English has created a new social class in Nigeria consisting of people who use English to mark their status. That aside, English is useful in helping to create a sense of unity in Nigeria's linguistic labyrinth.

A customer searches for local Hausa films known as Kannywood.

HAUSA

Hausa is the dominant language in northern Nigeria. Around 50 percent of the population speak Hausa as a first or second language. The Hausa are traditionally traders, and their language traveled with them wherever they went. Thus, people in neighboring states such as Kano or Borno began to speak Hausa. For a time, the Hausa empires extended as far as Yorubaland, and their language was known as far south.

Unlike Ibo or Yoruba, Hausa is a common language among all the people who call themselves Hausa. But Hausa has been affected by the other languages it has come into contact with. About a quarter of its vocabulary is Arabic in origin, while many words for handicraft skills or institutions are of Kanuri origin.

Hausa is a tonal language, and one word can have many shades of meaning, depending on the tone used in pronouncing the word. For example,

The native tongue of the Yoruba people is spoken, among other languages, in Nigeria, Benin, and Togo and in communities in other parts of Africa, Europe, and the Americas.

Living in central Nigeria between the Benue and Katsina rivers, the Tiv number more than 2.5 million people. They are an unusual group in that they speak a language that differs vastly from all the other languages of Nigeria. Tiv is closer in structure to the Bantu languages of southern Africa, which use several classifications of nouns, not simply masculine and feminine. The Tiv language that Tiv children learn in school uses a writing system developed by the early missionaries.

the word *kashi* can mean fighting, rain-soaked, heap, or excrement, so it is important to get the tone right.

FULFULDE

Fulfulde is the language spoken by Fulani pastoralists. While most Fulani have settled in Hausa settlements, speak Hausa, and look very much like Hausa people, the pastoral Fulani have maintained their language and their traditional nomadic lifestyle.

Hausa is spoken as a first language by about 25 million people, and as a second language by about 18 million more, a total of 43 million people.

Two Fulani junior high school students study at night in the yard of their home.

Fulfulde is unlike other languages of northern Nigeria. It is widely spoken, not just in Nigeria, since Fulani nomads travel all over Sudan, Niger, Burkina Faso, and Senegal. However, in each area the dialect is different, because it has been affected by the languages of the local people. Similar to Hausa, Fulfulde has adapted to local usage. Most pastoral Fulani speak two or three languages in order to communicate with the people on whose land they graze their cattle.

Fulfulde belongs to the Atlantic branch of the Niger-Congo language group and is related to languages spoken in Senegal. The more than 7 million Fulfulde speakers in Nigeria are dispersed in several states, including Bauchi, Borno, Kano, Katsina, and Sokoto. Each area has a different dialect, for example: Bororro, Kano-Katsina, and Sokoto.

The Fulani are traditionally a nomadic trading people, herding cattle, goats, and sheep across the vast dry hinterlands of their domain.

PIDGIN

In a country where hundreds of languages are spoken, there tends to be some highly creative linguistic innovation. Most Nigerians who have an elementary education possess a functional command of their indigenous language and English, and usually at least one more language.

Pidgin English enables people from different parts of Nigeria to communicate when they have no common language.

CODE SWITCHING

Nigeria's wide variety of languages has led to an interesting phenomenon called code switching. Nigerians slip from one language to another as they talk. Code switching is not unique to Nigeria. It happens in many languages. The French even have a national body that works to keep foreign words from entering their language, but most countries happily accept foreign words into their national language.

In Nigeria, code switching often occurs when topics change. Two people may be talking about a domestic topic in an indigenous language, but when they move to a technical or global topic, they subconsciously begin conversing in a different language, usually English. One reason is that many of the indigenous languages lack the vocabulary for certain subject areas. In other cases it might just seem proper to use a more formal language. Two people in an office might talk about their work in English but comment on the weather in Yoruba.

Nigerians may switch codes mid-sentence. For example, someone speaking in Yoruba to a person who is being too flippant will make the point by saying "you're wasting time" in English. Or they might add politeness to their speech with "please" or "thank you" in English.

A student reads and writes during English class.

Pidgin is a system of speech that develops to enable speakers of two different languages to communicate. In Nigeria pidgin must have begun when the European traders landed and bartered for slaves and oil. There is evidence of such roots in certain Nigerian pidgin words. For example, the word savvy could well have originated from the French *savez-vous*, meaning do you know, and been introduced by the French sailors who manned the ships.

Other examples of pidgin can be found in the Creole languages of the West Indies, which probably developed from the languages spoken by West African slaves who were brought to the islands.

Pidgin in Nigeria generally follows the grammatical rules of Ibo or Yoruba but uses English words. It is more widely spoken in the south of the country, where the traders first landed, and is used by uneducated people in ethnically mixed urban areas. It is also used by groups of southerners living in foreign enclaves in northern towns.

Nigerian pidgin is used in many primary schools where English has been introduced but not as the medium of instruction. One might make a comparison to *Krio*, a pidgin language in Sierra Leone, which is fast developing into an indigenous language.

The mass media in Nigeria sometimes uses pidgin. For example, in a newspaper article expressing disapproval of violence during elections, "We dun tire for wahallah in dis country" means "We are tired of political violence in this country."

A primary school student reading out loud during English class.

INTERNET LINKS

www.omniglot.com/writing/yoruba.htm

A description of the Yoruba language, together with learning materials and links to online Yoruba lessons, a Yoruba dictionary and Yoruba radio.

www.omniglot.com/writing/hausa.htm

A description of the Hausa language, together with learning materials and links to online Hausa lessons, Hausa dictionaries, and Hausa radio.

www.freelang.net/dictionary/fulfulde.php

A brief statement on the Fulfulde language today, with a free downloadable Fulfulde-English English-Fulfulde translator.

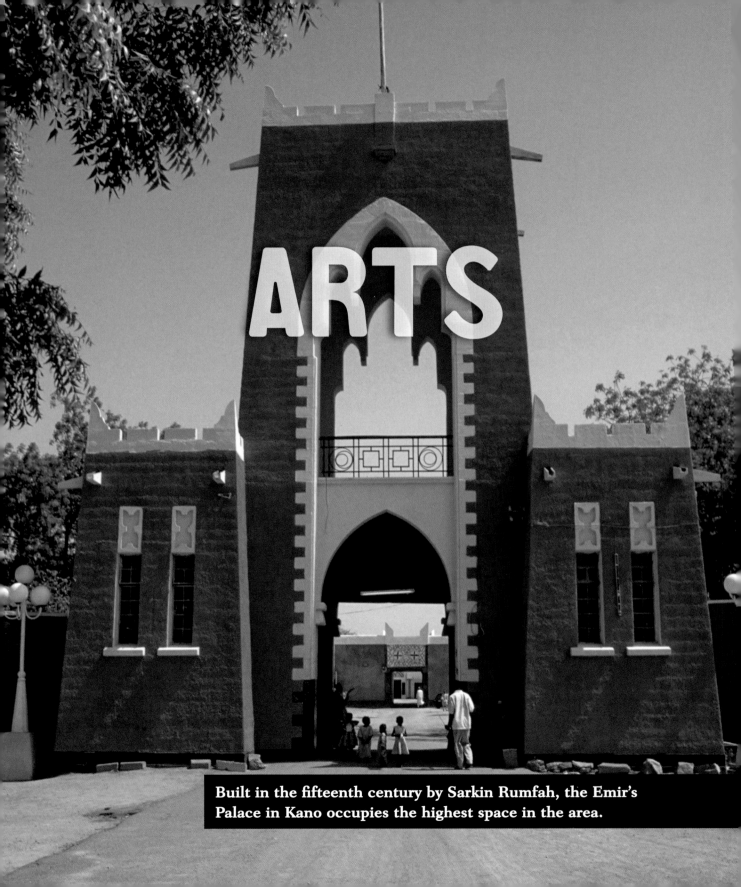

ARTS

Built in the fifteenth century by Sarkin Rumfah, the Emir's Palace in Kano occupies the highest space in the area.

10

LIKE MANY COUNTRIES with a colonial history, Nigeria has experienced tension between the demands of the local culture and those imposed by the foreign culture. Art is one area that has been influenced by the West. Traditional Nigerian art has always been functional. For instance, dance was related to social needs, teaching, and the rituals associated with village life.

An elaborately decorated house in Nigeria.

The culture of Nigeria is shaped by Nigeria's multiple ethnic groups. The country has over 50 languages and over 250 dialects and ethnic groups.

Nok terracotta statues are hollow and coil-built. Their features are highly stylized and they come in varying postures, often clad with jewelry.

Opposite: A bronze brass plaque from the 16th century showing the Oba of Benin with the attendants.

With the dominance of Western culture, many traditional art forms have lost their purpose and significance and have gone into decline. Many dances are no longer performed except in special shows, so the maskmakers' jobs are disappearing.

Western-style funerals are replacing the elaborate tombstones and burial plots of indigenous groups such as the Ibibio with organized city cemeteries. Instead of calabashes, people use plastic containers to store food. If a market still exists for the intricate leatherwork or pretty, woven cotton textiles of the northern states, it is because the rich are rediscovering their roots, or because of tourist demand for such items.

The government is aware that the nation's traditional arts are in decline. There has been an attempt to recover the traditional arts through festivals such as the All-Nigeria Festival of Arts. However, such festivals merely provide a platform to display the traditional dances, songs, and mimes. They have not revived the spirit of such art forms, which once celebrated the harvest of yams or the initiation of adolescents into adulthood, obsolete events in modern Nigeria.

EARLY ART FORMS

The oldest known works of art in Nigeria are the Nok terracotta statues, excavated from a site near the Jos Plateau. The statues date to 500 B.C. and were probably put in the fields to protect the crops. Regarded as art today, the Nok statues had a purely practical purpose when they were made.

Closer to the idea of art for its own sake are the bronze figures and plaques from the cities of Ife and Benin. The city of Ife, located in Oyo province in southwestern Nigeria, was once the capital of a kingdom established in the 11th century. Ife's artisans created bronze heads and terracotta statues. It is probable that the figures were used in rituals in which the figures of past kings would be paraded as a form of ancestor worship. The style of the figures is naturalistic, and they depict many details of dress and jewelry.

Benin succeeded Ife and by the 16th century had grown into a fine capital city. The kings of Benin commissioned bronze art works. At its height, Benin

CONTEMPORARY NIGERIAN ART

Traditional Nigerian art suffered when the country was part of the British Empire, because it was judged by Western standards. Used to the idea of art as something that uplifts and instructs the beholder, the Western art critic found Nigerian art primitive and in need of some of the sophistication of European art.

Modern Nigerian artists use European techniques to paint African subjects. Two pioneers were Aina Onabolu (1882—1963) and Akinola Lasekan (1916—72), who used conventional European portrait styles to paint Nigerian figures from a Nigerian perspective. Painter and sculptor Ben Enwonwu (1921—94) used African themes in all his works. Agbogho Mmuo, a series of paintings of an African masked dancer, won praise for visualizing rhythm in motion.

produced fine relief sculptures to decorate royal altars in ancestral rites. The wall plaques depicted symbolic motifs, scenes from court life, and historic events.

Images of frogs and crocodiles were used symbolically in Benin royal sculpture because of the animals' ability to live on land and in water. According to Benin beliefs, kings could move between the earthly and spiritual realms. Other Benin bronzes portrayed kings victorious in battle or their defeated enemies.

The city's work in bronze was equaled by its iron castings and ivory carvings. Today, many of the artifacts are housed in museums in Britain, taken there when the British robbed Benin of many of its art treasures in 1897.

The quality and technical skill of the kingdom's works of art had an enormous influence on the European art world. The Europeans were surprised to find such quality work in Africa, a place they considered primitive and undeveloped. Benin is still a center for the art of carving.

MUSIC

In Nigerian cultural tradition, music is intertwined with religion and can only be defined in the context of its role in rituals and festivals.

Different ethnic groups in Nigeria have different musical instruments, but there are some common elements. Rhythm is a very important component of Nigerian music. All groups make use of percussion instruments.

A tension drum is made from a piece of wood with animal skin stretched over its open top. The Hausa tension drum, called a *kalangu* (ka-LANG-oo), can reproduce some of the tonal elements of the Hausa language. The hourglass-shaped tension drum of the Yoruba, called a *dundun* (DOON-doon), varies in pitch and reproduces the sound of spoken Yoruba.

Besides their tension drum, the Ibo have a slit drum. It is made from a solid piece of wood that has been hollowed out in such a way that each side produces a different sound when struck. Technically, it is not a drum because it has no skin, but it is used in the same way that drums are used.

A local plays the traditional Nigerian tension drum.

Another traditional musical instrument is the xylophone, made from small pieces of wood that are struck to produce different musical notes. Other percussion instruments include gourd rattles, calabashes (for striking), thumb pianos, and harps.

But instruments are only a tiny aspect of traditional Nigerian music. Words are a major element, and they are sung not by an individual performer but by the whole community taking part in a celebration or festival. Tied to the music is dance and dress. The movements of the participants as they sing are complemented by their costumes and masks. Other elements associated with the music include figurines held above the dancers' heads, and fire.

Sakara (SAH-kah-rah) is an Islamic Yoruba style of music that originates from the traditional praise song of Yoruba society. It developed during the 1920s, when groups of musicians were paid to sing songs in praise of a particular political leader. *Sakara* is performed by men, led by a praise singer playing a *molo* (MCH-loh), a two-stringed lute. The praise singer leads the song, introducing new lines of verse as they occur to him or her, with the chorus following the lead, echoing the lines. *Sakara* has come to be performed at all Islamic religious festivals in Nigeria, such as the celebration marking a pilgrim's return from Mecca, the naming ceremony, weddings, and other events.

Asiko (AH-see-koh), the Christian version of *sakara*, has faster rhythms, and the musical instruments include drums, a carpenter's saw, and sometimes bottles. The lyrics are in Yoruba or pidgin and, as in *sakara*, use a call-and-response pattern.

Highlife music combines Western and traditional Nigerian styles. It borrows heavily from the West, with some local influences. Highlife can be described as the brass band and ballroom type of music that was popular during the 1930s and 1940s, with the added vitality of African rhythms.

DANCE

Traditional dance is vital to social life in rural Nigeria. Dance forms an integral component of religious ceremonies, such as coming-of-age, and a means of communicating with the gods or of choosing a potential marriage partner.

Traditional African dance rarely takes a form that Westerners identify with dancing. Traditionally, Nigerian men and women do not dance together. Nigerians were shocked when they first saw Western men and women making close body contact when they danced. Instead, Nigerian men and women dance in teams, and how well one dances might determine his or her prospects as a marriage partner.

A formal dance, such as that by a village association at a funeral, is performed by men wearing the carved masks and costumes associated with the appearance of a god in the village. In many cases, such dances are secret affairs, and women are banned from the meeting place when they are being performed.

Nigeria has been called "the heart of African music" because of its role in the development of West African highlife and palm-wine music, which fuses native rhythms with techniques imported from the Congo for the development of several popular styles that were unique to Nigeria.

Eyo masquerades
known as Adamu-
Orisha dance at
the Tafawa Balewa
Square in Lagos.
The Eyo festival
dates back to 1750
and takes place
whenever occasion
and tradition
demand, but it is
usually held as the
final burial rites for
a highly regarded
chief.

MASQUERADE

An essential part of the rituals that illuminate the rhythms of life in Nigeria is the masquerade. While in the past masquerades were performed for purposes of war, today they are performed mainly for entertainment. Masqueraders dance only at night, with a machete in hand and human skulls dangling from the waist. It is a sight designed to inspire courage against an enemy.

Another masquerade, also designed as a prelude to war, involves two figures: one of a man in a tight body stocking, carrying a carved wooden mask; and the other of a woman in a large velvet costume that is used to enhance the visual effect of the dance. But both dancers are men.

Often the masqueraders are not telling a particular story. Individual masqueraders represent different ancestors or gods and appear toward the end of a festival in a sudden and often frightening rush of activity. Parading masqueraders mime the actions of the deities they represent, but the actions of each masquerader have little bearing on the actions of the others.

LITERATURE

Nigeria has a rich literary tradition that predates the introduction of Western culture and literacy to the country.

Among the Igede people of Benue state, the Imwo Association exists to protect the interests of women. Its dances often express social criticism, particularly of overly aggressive men. An Igede women's association that performs at funerals uses bamboo clapping sticks as percussion. Igede women are not allowed to play drums or wear masquerade costumes.

Children in drumming families train in the art, and Oje children start training in traditional dance as soon as they can walk. They perform versions of traditional music and dance at social occasions.

Nigerian oral tradition originated in West African society. Nigeria's stories include stories about creation, stories about the gods, and stories about the origins of different groups of people. Such stories were crucial in preliterate times, because they were the people's means of keeping in touch with their past.

Nigeria's storytelling tradition has survived both literacy and slavery. Nigerian slaves shipped to other continents took many of their folktales with them. In the United States, for example, the stories of Br'er Rabbit have their origins in Nigerian oral tradition.

MODERN LITERATURE Wole Soyinka is probably the most famous modern Nigerian writer. He was born on July 13, 1934 near Abeokuta, the capital of Ogun state, and attended Ibadan University—Nigeria's first university—and then Britain's Leeds University.

Soyinka worked for a time in English theater and is well-known for his strong opposition to apartheid and military government. His works were banned in Nigeria for a period, and he spent time in jail during the Biafran War. He was awarded the Nobel Prize in Literature in 1986 and is perhaps most famous for plays such as *A Dance of the Forests*, *The Lion and the Jewel*, and *The Swamp Dwellers*.

Soyinka went into exile in 1994 and lived in the United States and Europe until 1998 when he returned to Nigeria.

Another famous Nigerian writer is Chinua Achebe, whose famous novel, *Things Fall Apart*, is well-known throughout the world. His novels address the problems of social disintegration caused by the massive changes sweeping Nigerian society.

For many Nigerian groups, children symbolize total innocence and purity, so some dances involve only small children or virgin girls.

A famous set of Nigerian stories originates from the Hausa people. The stories tell of a spider that was cleverer than all the other animals. In one story, God sent the spider to earth to fetch something but did not tell the spider what it was. The spider disguised itself and went back to heaven. It found out that it was to fetch the sun, the moon, and darkness and was also clever enough to return to earth and collect them. The spider thus proved its great skill and craftiness.

Fables that teach a moral to the listener are also popular among Nigerians. A Yoruba story tells how a wild goat refused to help the other animals keep their pond clean. The animals got angry with the goat and drove it away, so that it was forced ever after to live in the company of human beings.

The story of the antisocial goat demonstrates another function of storytelling in Nigeria: to pass on the family or clan's moral standards. The story of the goat not only teaches children to cooperate but also explains the existence of domestic goats.

"Nollywood", as the Nigerian movie industry is called, has emerged as the world's third largest producer of feature films. However, in comparison to Hollywood and Bollywood their movies are made within 10 days and at an average cost of around $15,000.

Other novelists who have taken up similar themes include Cyprian Ekwensi and Festus Iyayi, the latter in his excellent novel *Violence*. Another Nigerian author, Ben Okri, won the British Booker prize in 1991 for his surreal novel, *The Famished Road*. He has won several other literary awards, including the Paris Review and the Aga Khan prize.

Nigerian theater is equally rich. Besides the plays of Wole Soyinka in English, playwrights such as Fela Davies, Comish Ekiye, and Zulu Sofola write in both English and pidgin. The Ogunde theater, founded by Chief Herbert Ogunde, is an operatic form of stage play that combines Yoruba stories, dance, and music.

FILM

Nigeria has a flourishing film industry. Calpenny Productions, a Nigerian film company owned by Francis Oladele, produced Nigeria's first major feature film in 1971, *Kongi's Harvest*. It was based on the novel by Wole Soyinka, who also acted in the film. Other films made by the same company are *Bullfrog in*

the Sun, a joint venture with Germany and the United States. The first film in one of the indigenous languages was Amadi, a 1975 film made in Ibo.

In the Yoruban language, Ajani-Ogun incorporated aspects of Yoruban Theater into the medium of film, for the first time suggesting a completely new direction for Nigerian filmmaking. Other films made in the same idiom have been Black Goddess, a Portuguese language coproduction with Brazil, Orun Mooru, and Money Power.

ARCHITECTURE

Nigerian architectural styles vary from region to region, reflecting the needs of people in different terrains and climatic zones, ranging from humid swamps and forests to dry savanna land to hot desert.

The Ijo people of the Niger Delta have adapted their residential architecture to the natural environment they have lived in for centuries—open creeks and mangrove swamp, with very little dry land. Their houses are built on stilts

Born in Khana in the Niger Delta, Ken Saro Wiwa began his career as a government administrator and found his voice as an artist in his 40s, writing two novels, Songs in Time of War *(1985) and* Sozaboy *(1985), the latter in pidgin English, satirizing corruption in Nigerian society. In 1986 he wrote a collection of short stories called* A Forest of Flowers. *During the 1980s Wiwa also wrote a television series called* Basi and Company, *which became very popular.*

In the early 1990s Wiwa began to champion the Ogoni people of the Niger Delta in their opposition to environmental damage caused by the Shell oil company for which no compensation was made. In 1994 Wiwa and eight other Ogoni activists were arrested for their outspoken activism, tried by a special tribunal, and executed. The event aroused worldwide condemnation and resulted in Nigeria's expulsion from the British Commonwealth.

over the water, and the canoes they travel in often double as their home when the family has a long journey to make.

The stilts of the house are made from wood and are anchored in the riverbed. The stilts support a platform made from the same wood. The walls are made from bamboo and the roof from raffia palm. The porous walls and roof of the house are designed to allow fumes, heat, and smoke from inside to escape easily.

Just as the Ijo houses are appropriate to their natural landscape, so the Yoruba settlements reflect their way of life. Designed like a set of nested boxes, the arrangement of city, neighborhood, and house illustrates the social hierarchy of Yoruba life. The king's palace dominates the city; the neighborhood chief's house dominates the local square; and family courtyards are dominated by the quarters of the head of the house. Traditional Yoruba houses have walls made from mud bricks, and bamboo-thatched roofs overhang the courtyard to provide shelter from rain or sun for outdoor cooking and relaxation.

Similarly, Ibo architecture reflects the nature of their society. Houses are built in clusters rather than in extended family compounds. A central interior

Traditional circular Nigerian huts at a village between Sokoto and Kano.

column supports the roof, with exterior columns assisting. The walls are made of earth. Men's and women's houses are separate and designed to suit their function. The man's house has an inner room and an outer room; the latter designed for receiving guests.

In the north, the houses of Sokoto are built entirely from mud. They look like beehives, open at the top during the dry season and thatched during the wet season. The opening serves as a window and chimney.

Ancient monuments of Nigerian architecture are found in the city of Kano. They include the city's surrounding medieval walls and the Emir's palace, built in Hausa style. The Museum of Traditional Nigerian Architecture in Jos contains models of different Nigerian architectural styles.

INTERNET LINKS

www.onlinenigeria.com/music

Free Nigerian music to listen to by contemporary Nigerian singers/songwriters.

www.africatv24.com/music_video/nigeria

Authentic Nigerian Music Videos to watch and enjoy. An excellent microcosm of Nigerian culture.

www.pau.edu.ng/museum/#

Pan-African University's thrilling virtual tour of its museum of modern Nigerian art, with pictures of the artwork of contemporary Nigerian artists.

LEISURE

Soccer is a popular game among Nigerians, especially the youth.

MANY LEISURE ACTIVITIES enjoyed by people in developed countries have additional meaning when practiced by Nigerians. For example, people in a village in Nigeria dance not only for pleasure but to mark key events in the community. Similarly, in a society with no written language, storytelling and drama are more than entertainment; they pass on knowledge.

SPORTS

Soccer is a popular sport in Nigeria, and Nigerians play on several European teams. Stephen Keshi has spent his career playing for European teams, and Nwanko Kanu plays for Arsenal. Some other internationally known Nigerian soccer players are Julius Aghahowa, Isaac Okoronkwo, and Jay Jay Okocha.

Many traditional dances are exercises that improve the male performer's precision in movement and increase his fitness. Many traditional sports were geared toward the need for men to be fit, agile, and ready for warfare when the time came. Nigeria's war masquerades, for example, once served to test and increase the fitness and courage of warriors.

Among the Hausa, physical exercise reflects Islamic beliefs in the holiness of strength. The wrestling and boxing games that young men take part in are relics of a religion much older than Islam and based on fertility cults. In Hausa boxing matches, two young men bind their right hands and try to knock out their opponent.

ENJOYING STORIES

When rural Nigerians tell stories on a formal occasion, they may relate complete historical accounts accompanied by music and dance. Each night in the women's quarters, families sit and talk about their history or tell a moral tale that illustrates some preferred behavior. All Nigerian languages have proverbs that reveal the way people see the world and behave, and the proverbs are illustrated in their folktales.

In Ibo society two types of tales are typically told. One type concerns the history of a particular village, how it came to be, and who is related to whom. The other type of story is similar to a fairy tale and is usually a children's tale in which the characters are animals, rivers, the moon, or the sun. Ibo culture has a huge repertoire of proverbs that they retell whenever they want to illustrate or comment upon some event.

In a game often played by the Ibo, proverbs are paired. One player recites one proverb, and then the other player has to recite another proverb with a similar meaning.

Storytelling is part of daily life in Nigeria. A group of griots, such as the ones pictured above, usually call on a family to recite history through poetry, song and music.

In 1992 Nigeria had its first success in the Olympics. It won three silver medals in the men's 4x100 relay and in the heavyweight and super heavyweight boxing divisions, and a bronze in the women's 4x100 relay. However, Nigeria's greatest win was in soccer. The Nigerian team won a gold medal in the 1996 Summer Olympic Games when they defeated Argentina 3—2 to become the first African nation to win a gold medal in soccer (right). In the 2008 Olympic games held in Beijing, the Nigerian team won four medals. They did not secure a medal in the 2012 Olympics in London, but won a total of twelve medals, including six golds, at the Paralympics that same year.

The Hausa have just as many proverbs as the Ibo. One Hausa proverb, "Even the great river Niger must go round an island," means that power has limits. "A hare is not caught by sitting down" illustrates the Hausa respect for hard work, while "Before you tie up a hyena, think how you are going to let it go" encourages caution and forethought. The Hausa have a set of stories that they call dilemma tales. The stories have no ending, but they ask listeners what they would do or what judgment they would make under similar circumstances.

The Yoruba have invented many stories to explain the creation of the world. Here is one of them:

THE CREATION OF THE LAND Before there was the earth, there was a god called Odudwa, who went to the greatest god of all and asked for instructions. The supreme god told Odudwa to gather some chickens, some chameleons, and many chains. Then he gave Odudwa some sand, tied him to heaven by the chains, and lowered him down to earth.

There was no land to step on, so Odudwa sprinkled the sand onto the sea. Then he released a chameleon, and it delicately walked across the sand, one foot at a time. Then the chickens landed safely, and finally Odudwa went down to live on earth. Other gods later joined Odudwa one at a time.

That is how the earth was created and the chameleon got its delicate walk. Because of his bravery, Odudwa became the most important of the gods.

RESTFUL PURSUITS

After a gruelling day's work, many Nigerians like to enjoy restful activities in their leisure time. Television is a common item in most urban households as well as in the richer village homes.

The Hausa from the north have a saying, "Give a stranger water and listen to the news," which illustrates another popular Nigerian leisure activity—exchanging news. Visitors to Nigeria will find that people love to

Women in traditional Nigerian wear chatting by the road.

Afik was very proud and possessive of his wife. He followed her everywhere to make sure that no one else went near her.

Afik annoyed the people of the town so much that the town chief decided to teach him a lesson. The town chief offered a prize of a horse, a cloak, and 100,000 cowrie shells to anyone who could humiliate Afik by spending some time with his wife with Afik's knowledge.

A clever man named Musa had an idea. He took a seed case from a baobab tree and replaced the seeds with pieces of gold. He showed it to Afik and let Afik persuade him to show where the tree was.

Of course, Afik took his wife with him. When they got to the tree, Afik went up the ladder that they had brought with them.

While Afik was up in the tree, Musa removed the ladder. With Afik watching helplessly, Musa grabbed Afik's wife and kissed her, then left laughing to claim his prize.

After Musa left, Afik's wife put the ladder back against the tree so that Afik could climb down. But as he did so, the ladder slipped. Afik and the ladder fell on his wife, killing her.

Who was to blame for the death of Afik's wife? Afik, her jealous husband? Or Musa for his greed for the reward and his plan to shame Afik and his wife? Or the town chief, for offering such a reward in the first place?

listen to stories from around the world, and especially to stories from other parts of Nigeria.

Children's pastimes include playing games with friends in the evening after school or practicing one of many group dances that are performed at the harvest festival or at a wedding.

MEDIA IN NIGERIA

Nigeria's media scene is one of the most vibrant in Africa. State radio and TV have near-national coverage and operate at federal and regional levels. All 36 states run at least one radio network and a TV station.

By June 2010, 44 million Nigerians were online—around 29 percent of the population. Mobile phones are an important point of access to the web.

There are 100 radio stations and 147 terrestrial TV stations, as well as cable and direct-to-home satellite offerings. Radio is the most popular source of information. International broadcasters, including the BBC, are popular. However, rebroadcasts of foreign radio programs are banned.

Television is the second most popular medium. Viewing is concentrated in urban areas. Legislation limits the amount of foreign programming that stations can show, and outlets cannot air foreign news. The state TV says it reaches more than 90 million viewers. However, privately-owned Galaxy TV, Silver Bird TV, and AIT are the leading stations in some urban areas.

There are more than 100 national and local press titles, some of them state-owned.

LEISURE IN THE CITIES

Nigerian singer King Sunny Ade performs on stage.

In southern Nigerian cities, middle-class elite live alongside the very poor. In cosmopolitan Lagos and Ibadan, bars and nightclubs abound. Two popular local music forms, highlife and *juju*, are played in shabby bars around marketplaces and in sophisticated nightclubs patronized by the rich. In the northern cities, however, people lead a more traditional lifestyle and are less likely to spend their leisure time in clubs.

Highlife, the Nigerian version of Western big band, has assimilated African sounds. Greater emphasis has been given to rhythm than to melody, and a local percussion instrument called the *ekwe* (EK-way) is increasingly being used in place of trumpets or saxophones. Highlife music is full of social satire, similar to West Indian calypso.

Juju uses guitars of Western origin to produce rhythms similar to Yoruba rhythms. Popular Nigerian *juju* performers are Sunny Ade and Shina Peters. I. K. Dairowho, another well-known performer, has had streets named after him in Lagos and Ibadan.

VILLAGE SOCIETIES

Many societies exist in the villages for a variety of purposes. Some are aimed at the betterment of a particular group and their families, while others represent certain age groups in the village. A member of an age group can call on his peer group for help, and the peer group has the responsibility to provide the correct funeral rites when a member dies.

Many of Nigeria's village societies have secret handshakes and codes and keep secrets that they tell only to their society members. In the past, membership in a society might have required an act of bravery such as killing a wild animal. With wildlife conservation, however, the societies have a different membership requirement—high entry fees.

The village societies seek to help their members attain positions of power. That in turn increases the power and influence of the society.

In Ibo villages, societies operate as a credit association, forcing members to save and making loans when necessary.

INTERNET LINKS

www.allnigeriasoccer.com/
The complete Nigerian soccer portal—everything you could want to know about soccer in Nigeria.

www.motherlandnigeria.com/stories.html
Charming Nigerian stories and plays for children.

www.sacred-texts.com/afr/fssn/
Charming Folk Stories from Southern Nigeria with a moral included.

FESTIVALS

The Emir, or chief, riding a decorated horse at a Durbar festival in Maidugari. Celebrated at the culmination of Eid al-Fitr and Eid al-Adha, the day starts with prayers followed by a parade of the Emir, his entourage, and music players.

NIGERIA HAS MANY local festivals that date back to the time before the arrival of the major religions. They cover a wide range of events, from harvest festivals or betrothal festivals to a funeral or the investiture of a new chief.

It might seem odd to Western ways of thinking to celebrate funerals, but many Nigerians see death as a means of joining their ancestors, and so the deceased must get a good send-off.

Dances that were once performed by members of each village are now performed by professional troupes that tour villages to perform at local festivals.

The biggest festivals in the north celebrate events in the Islamic calendar. The end of the fasting month of Ramadan is followed 69 days later by Tabaski, a very colorful celebration. In northern towns such as Kano, Zaria, and Katsina, the Durbar performance has become a great tourist attraction. It is a procession in which the local leader, dressed in his finest and surrounded by a cavalry of finely dressed horsemen, parades through town on horseback. The procession includes other colorful figures such as wrestlers and musicians wearing headdresses made from feathers and cowry shells.

Festivals in the Christian calendar are celebrated mainly in the south. Christians in Nigeria include their indigenous religious rituals in the celebration of Christian festivals.

Sadly, in recent times, an extreme Islamist group, Boko Haram, has started a terror campaign against Christian institutions. On Christmas day 2011, the group bombed a Catholic Church in the capital city of

The three-day Argungu fishing festival, held on the banks of the Sokoto River in the town of Argungu, 64 miles (103 km) southwest of Sokoto, marks the end of the growing season and the start of the fishing season. A 1.2-mile (2-km) stretch of the Sokoto River is protected throughout the year, so that the fish will be plentiful for the 45-minute fishing frenzy in February or March.

More than 1,000 men armed with large gourds and hand nets compete for the fish in the river during the allotted time. Nile perch weighing up to 140 pounds (63.5 kg) are caught, and the biggest are offered to the local emirs who organize the festival.

The Argungu fishing festival began in the 1930s and has captured the nation's interest since. Apart from the main fishing event, there are canoe races, swimming and diving competitions, wrestling contests, handicraft displays, and traditional music and dance performances.

Abuja. The bombing killed 40 people. The group has pledged to drive all Christians out of northern Nigeria and institute Sharia Law in all areas of the country. Christians responded to the violence with prayer. In January 2012, 26 days after the deadly Christmas Day massacre, Boko Haram killed 185 people in a string of coordinated attacks. Churchgoers in Nigeria now pass through metal detectors and must navigate informal roadblocks set up to stop car bombers in order to attend Sunday church services. Boko Haram has claimed the lives of more than 480 people—both Christian and Muslim—as of May 2012 in Nigeria.

YORUBA FESTIVALS

Although the indigenous Yoruba religions have largely given way to Christianity and Islam, the traditional festivals are still celebrated. The traditional leader of the Yoruba, the Oba, lives in a palace and once governed with a council of ministers. The Oba's position is now mainly honorary, and his main role is as a special guest at festivals.

Traditional Yoruba festivals honor their pantheon of gods and mark the installation of a new Oba. The Engungun festival, which honors the ancestors, lasts seven days. Each day, an ancestor spirit represented by a possessed masked dancer parades through the town. On the last day, a priest goes to the shrine of the ancestors, sacrifices animals, and pours the blood on the shrine. The sacrifices are then collected and prepared for a feast.

THE SHANGO

The Yoruba call a rainmaker Shango. Held in July or August, the Shango festival honors Alaafin, an ancestor of the Oyo people who is believed to have become the god of thunder and lightning.

The Shango festival is celebrated for about 20 days. A priest makes sacrifices at the shrine of the thunder god. The town of Ife has a Yoruba art museum that displays some of the early earthen vessels used in the Shango festival.

On the last day of the Shango festival, the priest, possessed by the thunder god, eats fire and swallows gunpowder. Afterward, there is dancing and a feast with roast meat and palm wine at the Oba's palace.

The Yoruba priests were once rich and powerful but have lost much of their former wealth and power with the decline of the Oba's power and of the number of believers in the traditional gods.

THE BENIN FESTIVAL

The Benin festival takes place at the end of the rainy season, after the harvest has been gathered. It is partly a harvest festival but also serves another

In Iboland, for Christmas celebrations, the festivities include masquerade dancing, where men in their twenties or thirties dress in colorful costumes and wear masks. These masquerades, which pre-date the introduction of Christianity, honor the ancestral spirits.

THE IBO CELEBRATION OF ONITSHA IVORIES

Ibo society was originally centered on subsistence farming, so few Ibo became wealthy. Power in Ibo communities was based on the social standing of the person rather than the extent of his wealth.

But wealth has become important to the Ibo. While many of the old traditions are dying out, the Onitsha ivory festivals are celebrated more and more often.

The title of ivory holder can be claimed by any woman who has collected enough ivory and coral to make a costume. Usually, the participants are the wives of rich men, or women who have become successful in business and can buy their own ivory.

The participant has to have two huge pieces of ivory, one for each leg. The pieces might weigh up to 56 pounds (25 kg) each. In addition, two large pieces must adorn the wrists, and hundreds of dollars worth of coral and gold are worn as necklaces. Once she has accumulated the ivory, the participant must pay for a feast for as many people as possible. A special priest carries out a purification ceremony for the ivory.

The next stage of the process is even more elaborate. A woman with a full set of ivory ornaments can take the title of ozo (OH-zoh). In addition to the ivory, the expensive and elaborately embroidered white gown, and coral and gold ornaments, the participant must acquire an ivory trumpet and a horsetail switch.

Men can also take the title of ozo. When there is a ceremony for a new ozo, all similarly titled women and men dress up in their ivory ornaments and attend the celebration to mark the occasion.

purpose. Eligible young men and women of the village are ritually acquainted with one another.

Leboku is the name for the annual New Yam Festival celebrated in Ugep, Nigeria, in honor of the earth goddess and the ancestral spirits of the land.

The Benin festival is celebrated once every four years, and only the very wealthy can afford to have their children take part in the matchmaking ceremony. However, all the villagers get to enjoy the festive atmosphere.

Traditionally young girls who took part in the matchmaking ceremony would not wear any clothing, but in modern times, because nudity is frowned on, they are clothed. The main attractions of the girls' dress are the numerous heavy armlets and leg ornaments. They are so heavy that the girls must hold their arms over their heads during the ceremony in order to support the weight. Their hair is intricately plaited with coral beads.

Both boys and girls have elaborate markings painted on their bodies. The boys also take part in a tug-of-war as a demonstration of their strength.

OTHER FESTIVALS

Many communities celebrate a version of the harvest festival. In the south, it is often a new yam festival, held when the first of the season's yams are ready to eat.

Nigerians who live in the Niger Delta hold the Ikwerre, Kalabari, and Okrika festivals to celebrate the water spirits of their region. The masqueraders wear carved headdresses that resemble the heads of fish or water birds. Typically, a festival begins with a divination by the priest of the respective deity. Ritual sacrifices follow, then a song-and-dance performance depicting traits of the deity. The climax of the festival is usually a masquerader appearing disguised as the deity.

People in Finima celebrate the annual *Funfu Ma Tie*, a harvest festival that marks the break in the rainy season, so they can harvest their crops and start fishing. The costumed reveler wears a hat with nails attached at the ends and festival goers try to dodge these nails while being chased.

INTERNET LINKS

www.onlinenigeria.com/festivals/
All about the major festivals in Nigeria, including pictures.

www.skyscrapercity.com/showthread.php?t=859446
Spectacular photos of the various carnivals and festivals in Nigeria.

www.gowealthy.com/gowealthy/wcms/en/home/articles/ entertainment/events-and-festivals/Festivals-in-Nigeria- www.1AlyQEOKkE.html
A review of all the public holidays and festivals in Nigeria.

FOOD

Produce being sold at a busy market in Lagos.

THERE WAS A TIME when Nigeria was self-sufficient in its food supply, which was no mean feat for the largest nation—in terms of population size—on a continent that experienced frequent food shortages.

The oil boom had good and bad implications for Nigeria. While it earned a lot of foreign revenue, the emphasis on oil stole attention and resources from agriculture and made the country heavily dependent on foods such as milk, wheat, and sugar, which could easily have been produced domestically.

Nigerian cuisine uses spices and herbs together with palm oil or groundnut oil to create deeply flavored sauces and soups often made very hot with chilli peppers.

Sugarcane plants gathered at a market in Iddo.

Urbanization has supplemented or replaced traditional foods and cooking methods with Western influences or substitutes. In the cities, supermarkets and convenience stores sell processed foods, so that commuters on their way home after work can stop to pick up a quick dinner.

Nigerians have another alternative for meals on the go. Fast-food restaurants have grown in popularity since the 1980s, especially in the larger cities, such as Lagos, Abuja, and Port Harcourt. Many chains and outlets have tried to adapt their menus to local tastes. Wealthy Nigerians can enjoy fine dining in hotels and restaurants, which serve a variety of European, Asian, and other cuisines together with chilled wine.

Food staples vary from region to region. In the tropical south of the country, root vegetables such as yam, cocoyam, and sweet potato form the basis of a typical meal. Other subsistence crops grown in the south include rice, plantains, bananas, papayas, and pineapples.

Cattle bred and farmed in the north are sold and slaughtered in the south. Nigerians are switching from palm oil to peanut oil for cooking, although it is

Mr Bigg's is the largest fast food chain in Nigeria. Loosely modeled on McDonald's, they offer hamburgers and fries, as well as local fare.

2 teaspoons (10 ml) dried yeast

¾ cup (180 ml) warm water

1 pound (500 g) cornmeal flour

1 tablespoon (15 ml) cooking oil

Wild honey, as required

Dissolve the yeast in the water. Set aside until frothy. Mix in the cornmeal flour to make a batter of dripping consistency. Leave to rise for 30 minutes. Heat the oil in a small frying pan. Put a spoonful of the batter into the pan and fry slowly, turning once, so that it does not burn. Repeat until all the batter is used up. Serve with the honey.

more expensive, possibly because of the increasing wealth of people living in the cities and because of the availability of northern oil in southern markets.

DRINKS

Some of Nigeria's first light industries were breweries and soft-drink factories. Honey, sugarcane, and kola nuts form the basis of many drinks. Beer is popular. Palm wine, made in the south and sold in Lagos, gave its name to palm wine music, which was born in the clubs of Lagos. Palm wine can be fermented into an even stronger drink similar to gin. Alcohol is forbidden in Islam, although one of the largest breweries is in Kano, in the Islamic northern region.

THE SOUTHERN DIET

The southern Nigerian diet consists of the traditional foods of the major ethnic groups in the region, such as the Yoruba, Ibo, and Tiv.

The diet of the nomadic Fulani is based on milk and whatever grain they can buy in the areas where they trade.

A palm oil vendor sits with her child at a market in Lagos.

THE YORUBA DIET A typical Yoruba meal consists of two dishes: one of mashed vegetables or starchy dough made from corn or guinea corn; the other a stew made with chilies, tomatoes, green vegetables, and meat such as chicken, cooked in a base of palm oil, flavored with onions, and thickened with ground nuts. The meal is finished with fruit. *Gari* (GA-ree) is another traditional Yoruba dish. It is made from cassava root, which is pounded and then boiled or fried.

THE IBO DIET The typical range of foods available to the Ibo includes cassava, cocoyam, and a kind of potato called edo. Beans, corn, okra, pumpkin, and peanuts are also eaten. Bananas, coconuts, mangoes, oranges, plantains, and papayas sweeten the diet and provide vitamins.

THE TIV DIET The basis of the main Tiv meal is a loaf made from yams, millet, or sorghum. To eat the loaf, a Tiv person breaks off a piece, rolls it into a ball, moulds it until it becomes spoon-shaped, and dips it into a sauce that is made with meat, green vegetables, and palm oil. Typical of Tiv cooking is the use of sesame as a spice.

THE NORTHERN DIET

Suya is a meat kebab coated with ground peanuts, chili pepper, and other local spices. It is prepared barbecue-style on a stick.

Similarly, the northern diet consists of the traditional foods of ethnic groups in the region, such as the Hausa and Fulani. Peanut oil is more commonly used than palm oil.

THE HAUSA DIET Ground millet, sorghum, or corn forms the basis of a traditional Hausa meal. The grains are boiled into a porridge called *tuwo* (TOO-woh), which is eaten with a sauce that is made from onions, okra, tomatoes, and meat. Meat is usually reserved for special occasions.

KOLA NUTS

The nut of the kola fruit is the main ingredient in soft drinks. The fruit is like a large grapefruit and grows on trees. When it is fully ripe, the green skin peels away, revealing the silver and pink nuts inside. The nuts are crushed to produce the juice used in cola drinks. Nigerians chew the nuts, which contain a mild alcoholic stimulant, to quench their thirst. To give someone a kola nut is a sign of friendship.

THE FULANI DIET Largely settled and working as herders for the wealthier Hausa, the Fulani depend on grain that they buy from areas where they trade, and milk from the cattle raised by their wealthy employers. The Fulani rarely eat meat, since that would require the slaughter of cattle. The nomadic Fulani raise cattle as a source of beef and milk, which they use in trade.

KITCHENS AND COOKING UTENSILS

Few countries have the wide variety of ordinary cooking methods that Nigeria has. The nomadic Fulani's kitchen consists of only the essentials that can be carried by their pack oxen. That includes a receptacle such as a calabash to store milk, an earthenware pot for cooking grain, and an iron tripod to balance the pot over the fire. When the family settles in a camp, an open fire in the women's quarters of the compound becomes the kitchen.

An African woman cooking with her daughters in a traditional camp in northern Nigeria.

In traditional Hausa homes, the cooking area is in a covered porch in the women's section. Each wife has her own kitchen, usually a cooking place with an open fire. There is a piped water supply in the towns, but families in more rural areas get their water from a well in the courtyard, or a communal well outside the courtyard. Most water outside the larger towns is not suitable for drinking.

A similar arrangement applies in Yoruba settlements. Cooking is done in the open courtyard unless the weather is bad. Then people cook indoors, and the smoke filters out through spaces in the roof.

Such kitchens exist in villages or small towns. In the larger towns, the households of lower-paid workers have similarly equipped kitchens. Kitchens in the wealthier suburbs of the cities have modern appliances such as food processors, microwave ovens, and dishwashers.

TABOOS, CUSTOMS, AND ETIQUETTE

Dining the traditional Nigerian way does not require the use of utensils. Food is served in straw baskets, and people eat using their fingers.

Modern Nigerians use imported plastic or metal utensils that are sold in the markets. In the towns Western-style china and flatware are used in wealthy households, while people in the villages use both traditional and modern implements.

Nigerian etiquette requires that elders be served first, and only after they have finished are the other members of the family allowed to eat what food is left. That practice gave rise to a popular Nigerian proverb, "The elder who eats all his food will carry his load by himself."

Vendors in the open air market in Maiduguri.

BUYING GROCERIES

The small market is a vital part of Nigerian life. Whereas in the West the direct relationship between consumer and producer has been replaced by large-scale marketing, in Nigeria the small market is still where most people buy essential foodstuffs.

Even in the larger cities, where supermarkets sell processed food, which has become a status symbol for the rich, the marketplace still beckons as the best place to get the freshest and cheapest meat and vegetables and to catch up on the local news.

With modernization and improved transportation, Nigerians are no longer limited in their choices of ingredients to what can be grown or raised locally. In the past, there was little beef available in the south because of the prevalence of the tsetse fly. The fly is a carrier of African trypano-somiasis, or sleeping sickness, of which cattle can be carriers or victims. Trypano-somiasis can spread to human beings and end cattle-raising activity.

INTERNET LINKS

www.allnigerianrecipes.com/

The Nigerian food website to go to. Has recipes for every single type of Nigerian food imaginable, together with cooking videos and cooking tips.

www.food.com/recipes/nigerian

Has Nigerian recipes classified into various categories such as Quick and Easy, Recommended, Healthy, etc. A convenient site for anyone wanting to try out Nigerian cuisine.

http://recipes.wikia.com/wiki/Nigerian_Cuisine

Nigerian recipes, together with a glossary, preparation methods, special equipment needed, and a special category of Nigerian food traditions and festivals.

Fossilized tsetse flies have been recovered from the Florissant Fossil Beds in Colorado, laid down some 34 million years ago. There are 23 species of tsetse flies. Diseases transmitted by tsetse flies kill 250,000 to 300,000 people per year.

JOLLOF FRIED RICE

This versatile dish is found throughout West Africa and is commonly served with fried chicken and fried sliced plantains. Makes 4 servings.

¼ cup (60 ml) vegetable oil

1 medium onion, sliced

2 medium tomatoes, sliced

1 medium red pepper, diced

4 tablespoons (60 ml) tomato purée

½ tablespoon (7.5 ml) curry powder

pinch of thyme

pinch of cayenne pepper

1 bay leaf

salt and pepper to taste

2 cups (500 ml) water

1 stock cube

1 cup (250 ml) long-grained rice

In a large saucepan on medium heat, heat the oil and fry the onions until translucent. Stir in the tomatoes, red pepper and tomato purée and season with curry powder, thyme, cayenne pepper, the bay leaf, salt, and pepper. Add the water and stock cube then bring to a boil. Add the rice, cover and simmer on low heat for 20 to 30 minutes, or until the rice is cooked. Serve with fried plantains and a green salad.

PUFF PUFFS (NIGERIAN SWEET PUFFS)

This fried shortcrust pastry comes in different shapes for different festivals or special occasions. Makes 4 servings.

2 cups (500 ml) plain flour

2 teaspoons (10 ml) yeast

½ teaspoon (2.5 ml) salt

4 tablespoons (60 ml) butter

4 tablespoons (60 ml) fine granulated sugar

½ teaspoon (2.5 ml) ground nutmeg

400ml of water, lukewarm

Vegetable oil, for frying

Sift the flour and salt together in a bowl, add the the sugar and nutmeg. Rub in the butter. Make a well in the center of the mixture. Pour the water, little by little, into the well until the batter is smooth (but not watery) and without lumps. Flatten the dough using a rolling pin on a lightly floured chopping board. Cover the bowl with a clean dry cloth or aluminum foil and leave the batter to rise for about 45 to 50 minutes. Heat the oil in a pan, scoop the batter into your palm and drop into the oil by pressing the batter between your thumb and your fore finger. Fry until brown, take out and drain away the excess oil on paper towels. Serve warm.

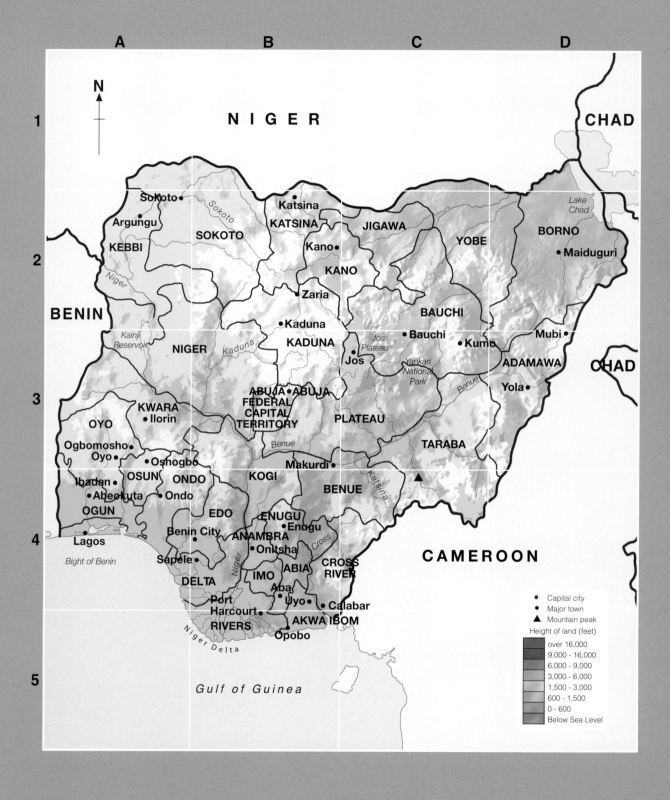

MAP OF NIGERIA

ECONOMIC NIGERIA

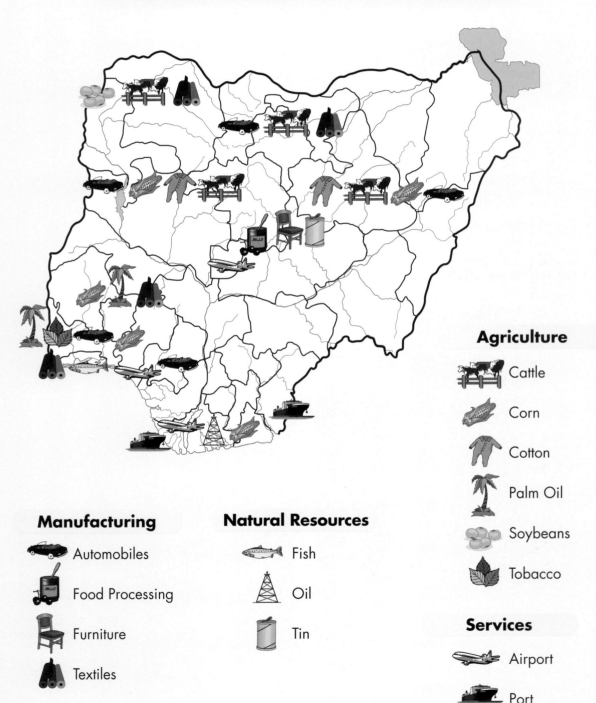

Agriculture

- Cattle
- Corn
- Cotton
- Palm Oil
- Soybeans
- Tobacco

Services

- Airport
- Port

Manufacturing

- Automobiles
- Food Processing
- Furniture
- Textiles

Natural Resources

- Fish
- Oil
- Tin

ABOUT THE ECONOMY

OVERVIEW

Oil-rich Nigeria has been hobbled by political instability, corruption, inadequate infrastructure, and poor macroeconomic management but in 2008 began pursuing economic reforms. Since 2008 the government has begun to show the political will to implement the market-oriented reforms urged by the International Monetary Fund (IMF), such as modernizing the banking system, removing subsidies, and resolving regional disputes over the distribution of earnings from the oil industry. GDP rose strongly between 2007 and 2012 due to the of growth in non-oil sectors and robust global crude oil prices.

GROSS DOMESTIC PRODUCT (GDP)

US$455.5 billion
Per capita: $2,300 (2012 estimate)

GROWTH RATE

6.3 percent (2012 estimate)

INFLATION RATE

12.2 percent (2012 estimate)

CURRENCY

1 Nigerian naira (NGN) = 100 kobo
USD 1 = 160.3 NGN (October 2013)
Notes: 5, 10, 20, 50, 100, 200, 500 & 1000 naira
Coins: ½, 1, 5, 10, 25, 50 kobo, 1 & 2 naira

EXTERNAL DEBT

$13.12 billion (2012 estimate)

WORKFORCE

53.83 million (2012 estimate)

UNEMPLOYMENT RATE

23.9 percent (2011 estimate)

POPULATION BELOW POVERTY LINE

70 percent (2010 estimate)

INDUSTRIES

Crude oil, coal, tin, columbite; rubber products, wood; hides and skins, textiles, cement and other construction materials, food products, footwear, chemicals, fertilizer, printing, ceramics, steel

AGRICULTURAL PRODUCTS

Cocoa, peanuts, cotton, palm oil, corn, rice, sorghum, millet, cassava, yams, rubber; cattle, sheep, goats, pigs; timber; fish

NATURAL RESOURCES

arable land, coal, iron ore, lead, limestone, natural gas, niobium, petroleum, tin, zinc

MAJOR EXPORTS

Petroleum and petroleum products (95 percent of exports), cocoa, rubber

MAJOR IMPORTS

Machinery, chemicals, transport equipment, manufactured goods, food and live animals

MAJOR TRADING PARTNERS

The United States, China, India, Netherlands, Brazil, Spain, France, UK

CULTURAL NIGERIA

Fishing Festival
The highlight of the three-day festival at Argungu is the fishing competition. Participants enter the Sokoto River with hand nets to catch the largest fish.

Emir's Palace
The Emir's palace at Kano is a famous monument built in ancient Hausa architectural style.

Nok Statues
Terracotta statues excavated in the Jos Plateau region date back to the Nok civilization more than 1,500 years ago.

Lake Chad
Tourists can ride boats on Lake Chad and visit fishing villages on its shores. However, the lake is shrinking due to a drying climate and an increasing demand for water in Cameroon, Chad, Niger, and Nigeria.

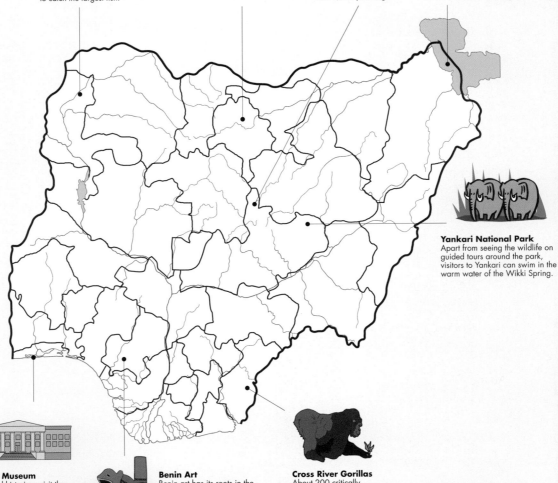

Yankari National Park
Apart from seeing the wildlife on guided tours around the park, visitors to Yankari can swim in the warm water of the Wikki Spring.

National Museum
Tourists and historians visit the national museum in Lagos to see one of the country's widest ranges of ancient art works, such as the Nok statues.

Benin Art
Benin art has its roots in the bronze sculptures that depicted the life and battles of the former kingdom.

Cross River Gorillas
About 200 critically endangered gorillas live in isolated groups in the Cross River National Park.

ABOUT THE CULTURE

OFFICIAL NAME
Federal Republic of Nigeria

CAPITAL
Abuja

NATIONAL FLAG
Three equal vertical bands of green (hoist side), white, and green; the color green represents the forests and abundant natural wealth of the country, white stands for peace and unity

AREA
356,669 square miles (923,768 square km)

MAJOR CITIES
Lagos, Ibadan, Kaduna

PROVINCES
Abia, Adamawa, Akwa Ibom, Anambra, Bauchi, Bayelsa, Benue, Borno, Cross River, Delta, Eboryi Edo, Ekiti, Enugu, Federal Capital Territory, Gombe, Imo, Jigawa, Kaduna, Kano, Katsina, Kebbi, Kogi, Kwara, Lagos, Nassarawa, Niger, Ogun, Ondo, Osun, Oyo, Plateau, Rivers, Sokoto, Taraba, Yobe, Zamfara

POPULATION
174.5 million (2013 estimate)

POPULATION GROWTH
2.54 percent (2013 estimate)

ETHNIC GROUPS
Of the more than 250 groups, the largest are the Hausa and Fulani (29 percent), the Yoruba (21 percent), and the Ibo (18 percent), Ijaw 10 percent, Kanuri 4 percent, Ibibio 3.5 percent, Tiv 2.5 percent.

OFFICIAL LANGUAGES
English (official), Hausa, Ibo, Yoruba, Fulfulde, and hundreds of other indigenous languages

MAJOR RELIGIONS
Islam 50 percent, Christianity 40 percent, indigenous beliefs 10 percent

LIFE EXPECTANCY
52.46 years (2013 estimate)

BIRTH RATE
38.78 births/1,000 population (2013 estimate)

DEATH RATE
13.2 deaths/1,000 population (2013 estimate)

INFANT MORTALITY RATE
72.97 deaths/1,000 live births (2013 estimate)

LITERACY RATE
61.3 percent of adults more than 15 years old can read and write (2010 estimate)

TIMELINE

IN NIGERIA	IN THE WORLD

800 B.C.–A.D. 200
Nok culture dominates the Jos Plateau.

1486
Portuguese explorer João Affonso d'Aveiro arrives in Benin.

1570–1600
The Kanem-Borno Empire peaks.

1804
The first of several holy wars that will establish a Fulani empire centered on Sokoto.

1861
Britain occupies Lagos.

1897
Many royal art works are stolen from Benin.

1914
The British merge the north and south into a single protectorate.

1939
Nigeria is split into three regions: north, east, and west.

1946
A new constitution shifts power from the central government to the regions.

1954
Nigeria is made an autonomous federation.

1960
Britain grants independence.

1966
Two military coups lead to Ibo massacres.

1967–70
The Biafran War

1975
Murtala Muhammad stages a coup. Plans begin for the new capital city, Abuja.

1976
Muhammad is assassinated; Olusegun Obasanjo succeeds him.

1979
Shehu Shagari assumes the presidency, ending 13 years of military rule.

1993
Sani Abacha seizes power and suppresses political opposition.

1995
Execution of Ken Saro Wiwa and other human rights activists; the British Commonwealth expels Nigeria.

1206–1368
Genghis Khan unifies the Mongols and starts conquest of the world. At its height, the Mongol Empire under Kublai Khan stretches from China to Persia and parts of Europe and Russia.

1776
U.S. Declaration of Independence

1914
World War I begins.

1939
World War II begins.

1945
The United States drops atomic bombs on Hiroshima and Nagasaki. World War II ends.

IN NIGERIA		IN THE WORLD
1998 Abacha dies. Abdulsalam Abubakar succeeds him and frees political prisoners.		**1997** Hong Kong is returned to China.
1999 Obasanjo is elected president. The Commonwealth readmits Nigeria. Several northern states establish Islamic law.		
		2001 Terrorists crash planes into New York, Washington D.C., and Pennsylvania.
2003 Obasanjo wins the election to serve as president for a second consecutive term.		**2003** War in Iraq begins.
2004 State of emergency is declared in the central Plateau State after Muslims are killed in Yelwa in attacks by Christian militia; revenge attacks are launched by Muslim youths in Kano.		**2004** Eleven Asia countries are hit by giant tsunami, killing at least 225,000 people.
2005 The Paris Club, an informal group from the world's biggest economies, agrees to write off two-thirds of Nigeria's $30b foreign debt.		**2005** Hurricane Katrina devastates the Gulf Coast of the United States.
2006 Helped by record oil prices, Nigeria becomes the first African nation to pay off its debt to the Paris Club of rich lenders.		
2007 Umaru Yar'Adua of the ruling People's Democratic Party is proclaimed winner of the presidential election.		
2008 Oil trades at $100 a barrel for the first time.		
2009 Security forces kill Boko Haram's leader for launching a campaign of violence in a bid to impose Sharia law on the entire country.		**2009** Outbreak of flu virus H1N1 around the world
2010 President Umaru Yar'Adua dies. Vice-president Goodluck Jonathan, already acting in Yar'Adua's stead, succeeds him.		
2011 Goodluck Jonathan wins presidential election.		**2011** Twin earthquake and tsunami disasters strike northeast Japan, leaving more than 14,000 dead and thousands more missing.
2012 Unions suspend action over government's decision to drop fuel subsidies.		
2013 Preparations begin for the West Africa regional conference of the World Federation of Consuls (FICAC) in March 2014.		

GLOSSARY

Biafra
A region of eastern Nigeria that tried to secede in the civil war of 1967 to 1970.

bicameral (bahy-KAM-er-uhl)
Having two branches, chambers, or houses, as a legislative body.

dundun **(DOON-doon)**
An hourglass-shaped tension drum that produces sounds similar to those in Yoruba speech.

Fulani
A pastoral Muslim people of western Africa.

Fulfulde
The language of the Fulani people.

gele **(GAY-lay)**
A head tie worn by Yoruba women.

harmattan (har-mat-TAN)
A winter wind that blows from the Sahara Desert toward northern Nigeria.

Hausa
The main ethnic group in northern Nigeria; also the language of the Hausa people.

highlife
Nigeria's version of big band music. It is rhythmic and uses African instruments.

Ibo
The main ethnic group in southeastern Nigeria; also the language of the Ibo people.

Kanem-Borno
An early Islamic civilization in northern Nigeria.

obeche (oh-BEE-chee)
A large African tree with light-colored wood.

Oyo
A Yoruba kingdom in southwestern Nigeria that developed from the 14th century.

shadoof
An ancient water-raising device still used in some areas of Nigeria. It has a weight at one end of a rod balances a bucket at the other end.

Sokoto
The center of the 19th-century Fulani Empire; also a state in present-day northwestern Nigeria, and the capital of that state.

suffrage (SUHF-rij)
The right to vote, especially in a political election.

tsetse fly
A fly that carries trypano-somes, which cause a disease called trypano-somiasis, also known as sleeping sickness, among animals and people.

Yoruba
The main ethnic group in southwestern Nigeria; also the language of the Yoruba people.

FOR FURTHER INFORMATION

BOOKS

Adichie, Chimamanda Ngozi. *Half of a Yellow Sun*. Harpswell, ME: Anchor, 2007.

Campbell, John. *Nigeria: Dancing on the Brink* (Council on Foreign Relations Books). Lanham, MD: Rowman & Littlefeld, 2010.

Cunliffe, Jones. *My Nigeria: Five Decades of Independence*. New York: Palgrave Macmillan, 2010.

Falola, Toyin and Heaton, Matthew M. *A History of Nigeria*. Cambridge, UK: Cambridge University Press, 2008.

Gordon, April and Elliot Barker. *Nigeria's Diverse Peoples: A Reference Sourcebook*. Santa Barbara, California: ABC-CLIO, 2003.

Lemieux, Diane. *Nigeria—Culture Smart! The Essential Guide to Customs & Culture*. London: Kuperard, 2012.

Okonjo, Chukuka. *Nigeria in the First Decade of the 21st Century*. Ibadan, Nigeria: Spectrum Books, 2000.

Peel, Michael. *A Swamp Full of Dollars, Pipelines and Paramilitaries at Nigeria's Oil Frontier*. Chicago: Lawrence Hill Books, 2010.

Smith, Daniel Jordan. *A Culture of Corruption: Everyday Deception and Popular Discontent in Nigeria*. New Jersey: Princeton University Press, 2008.

Uzokwe, Alfred Obiora. *Surviving in Biafra: The Story of the Nigerian Civil War*. Kosciusko, Mississippi: Writer's Advantage, 2003.

DVDS

Pilot Productions: *Globe Trekker—Nigeria*. Pilot Productions, May 2011.

IROK Solutions, Inc. *Flavors of Africa Cooking DVD—Kenya, Nigeria & South Africa,* IROK Solutions, Inc., September 2007.

MUSIC

Various Artists. *Wyld Pytch/51 Lex Records Presents: Music From Nigeria*. Wyld Pytch Rekords, 2009 51 Lex Records.

Various Artists. *Nigeria 70 Sweet Times: Afro-Funk Highlife*. STRUT RECORDS, 2011.

Various Artists. *Nigeria Special: Modern Highlife, Afro-sounds & Nigerian Blues 1970-76*, Soundway Records Ltd, 2008 Soundway.

BIBLIOGRAPHY

BOOKS

Achebe, Chinua. *The Trouble With Nigeria*. Enugu: Fourth Dimension Publishing Co., 2000.

Achu, Kamala. *Nigeria*. New York: Franklin Watts, 1992.

Awde, Nicholas. *Hausa-English English-Hausa Dictionary*. Hippocrene Practical Dictionary series. New York: Hippocrene Books, 1996.

de Grunne, Bernard. *The Birth of Art in Africa: Nok Statuary in Nigeria*. Paris, France: Vilo International, 1999.

Ezra, Kate. *Royal Art of Benin: The Perls Collection in the Metropolitan Museum of Art*. New York: Metropolitan Museum of Art, 1992.

Okri, Ben. *The Famished Road*. Peterborough, UK: Anchor Books, 1993.

Peil, Margaret. *Lagos: The City Is the People*. Thorndike, Maine: GK Hall & Co., 1991.

Saro-Wiwa, Ken and William Boyd. *A Month and a Day: A Detention Diary*. New York: Penguin, 1996.

Schultz, John Frederick (editor). *Nigeria ... in Pictures (Visual Geography series)*. Minneapolis, Minnesota: Lerner Publications Company, 1995.

WEBSITES

allAfrica.com:Nigeria. http://allafrica.com/nigeria/

All Nigerian Recipes.com. www.allnigerianrecipes.com/

All Nigeria Soccer.com. http://allnigeriasoccer.com/

BBC News Timeline: Nigeria. http://news.bbc.co.uk/2/hi/africa/country_profiles/1067695.stm

BribeNigeria.com—Fighting Corruption in Nigeria. www.bribenigeria.com/

Central Intelligence Agency World Factbook (select Nigeria from the country list). www.cia.gov/cia/publications/factbook

Commonwealth Network—Nigeria. www.commonwealth-of-nations.org/Nigeria/Government/Government_Ministries

Economy Watch—Nigeria's Economy. www.economywatch.com/world_economy/nigeria/

Fulfulde-English dictionary. www.freelang.net/dictionary/fulfulde.php

Motherland Nigeria. www.motherlandnigeria.com

NigeriaWorld.com—All about Nigeria. www.nigeriaworld.com/

Online Nigeria. www.onlinenigeria.com/

Pan-African University—Virtual Museum of Modern Nigerian Art. www.pau.edu.ng/museum/#

The Fattening Room. www.maobongoku.com/maobong_mypeople_tradition_fattening.htm

United Nations Environment Program—Nigeria. www.unep.org/nigeria/

US Department of State—History of Nigeria. www.state.gov/r/pa/ei/bgn/2836.htm#history.

Women for Women.org—Women of Nigeria. www.womenforwomen.org/global-initiatives-helping-women/help-women-nigeria.php

INDEX

INDEX